CAMBRIDGE LIBRARY COLLECTION

Books of enduring scholarly value

Music

The systematic academic study of music gave rise to works of description, analysis and criticism, by composers and performers, philosophers and anthropologists, historians and teachers, and by a new kind of scholar - the musicologist. This series makes available a range of significant works encompassing all aspects of the developing discipline.

Mendelssohn

The composer, virtuoso pianist and conductor Felix Mendelssohn (1809–47) was lionised by the music-loving public during his lifetime, and his music is still greatly admired today. A versatile child prodigy, he wrote music for *A Midsummer Night's Dream* while he was still a teenager. Masterpieces such as the octet for strings, the 'Italian' symphony, the violin concerto and his great oratorio *Elijah* followed. His extraordinary ability was such that he was made an honorary member of the Philharmonic Society in 1829 at the age of only twenty during the first of his ten visits to Britain. A great advocate of Johann Sebastian Bach, Mendelssohn did much to reawaken interest in his music. This eminently readable short biography by the composer William Smith Rockstro (1823–95) was first published in 1884 as part of Francis Hueffer's 'Great Musicians' series. A list of Mendelssohn's works is included as an appendix.

T0345440

Cambridge University Press has long been a pioneer in the reissuing of out-of-print titles from its own backlist, producing digital reprints of books that are still sought after by scholars and students but could not be reprinted economically using traditional technology. The Cambridge Library Collection extends this activity to a wider range of books which are still of importance to researchers and professionals, either for the source material they contain, or as landmarks in the history of their academic discipline.

Drawing from the world-renowned collections in the Cambridge University Library and other partner libraries, and guided by the advice of experts in each subject area, Cambridge University Press is using state-of-the-art scanning machines in its own Printing House to capture the content of each book selected for inclusion. The files are processed to give a consistently clear, crisp image, and the books finished to the high quality standard for which the Press is recognised around the world. The latest print-on-demand technology ensures that the books will remain available indefinitely, and that orders for single or multiple copies can quickly be supplied.

The Cambridge Library Collection brings back to life books of enduring scholarly value (including out-of-copyright works originally issued by other publishers) across a wide range of disciplines in the humanities and social sciences and in science and technology.

Mendelssohn

WILLIAM SMITH ROCKSTRO

CAMBRIDGE
UNIVERSITY PRESS

University Printing House, Cambridge, CB2 8BS, United Kingdom

Published in the United States of America by Cambridge University Press, New York

Cambridge University Press is part of the University of Cambridge.
It furthers the University's mission by disseminating knowledge in the pursuit of
education, learning and research at the highest international levels of excellence.

www.cambridge.org
Information on this title: www.cambridge.org/9781108061186

© in this compilation Cambridge University Press 2013

This edition first published 1884
This digitally printed version 2013

ISBN 978-1-108-06118-6 Paperback

The Great Musicians

Edited by Francis Hueffer

MENDELSSOHN

By W. S. ROCKSTRO

AUTHOR OF "THE LIFE OF HANDEL,"
"A HISTORY OF MUSIC FOR YOUNG STUDENTS," ETC., ETC.

LONDON

SAMPSON LOW, MARSTON, SEARLE, AND RIVINGTON

CROWN BUILDINGS, 188, FLEET STREET

1884

CONTENTS.

—◆◇◆—

CHAPTER I.

CONTENTS.

MENDELSSOHN.

—◇◇—

CHAPTER I.

THE FOUNDER OF THE FAMILY.

AMONG the once celebrated but now almost forgotten
Art-centres of northern Europe, the nurseries of Song,
the *foci* whence, from time to time, bright flashes of
creative genius have radiated far and wide, few have
laid the world under deeper obligations than sober,
business-loving Hamburg. When German Opera was
in its infancy, the inhabitants of the old Hanse town
fostered its early efforts with a well-directed zeal which
soon led to its acceptance as an independent mani-
festation of inventive power. The earliest Singspiel
that was ever publicly performed in the German
language—Johann Theile's *Adam und Eva*—was
first produced at Hamburg, in 1678. Here, fourteen years later, the wealthy merchants of the north-
east frontier built themselves a Theatre, in the busy
Gänsemarkt, and flocked to it in crowds to hear

B

the Operas of Strunck, and Franck, and Conradi, and
valiant Reinhard Keiser. Here Handel produced *Al-
mira*, and *Nero*, and *Daphne*, and *Clorindo;* and set to
music the Passion-poem of Brockes, as Keiser and
Telemann had done before him; and laid the first
foundation of his world-wide fame. Here Mattheson
invented the art of musical criticism; or, at least, invested it with so new and powerful an interest that he
may fairly be said to have first breathed into it the
breath of life. And here, on Friday, the 3rd of February,
1809, was born, at No. 14 in the Grosse Michælisstrasse,
one of the brightest musical geniuses of the present
century, Jakob Ludwig Felix Mendelssohn-Bartholdy,
the subject of our present memoir.

The question of the hereditary transmission of genius
is a vexed one; supported on the one side, and negatived
on the other, by evidence of the most contradictory
character. The history of the Bach family, for instance,
would lead us to a conclusion very different to that
suggested by general observation. But on one point
there is no doubt. Whatever may be the case with regard to special manifestations of artistic power, it is quite
certain that intellectual capacity, in its abstract form, is
transmissible from father to son in unlimited measure,
and, in certain cases, waits only to unite itself with some
definite inspiration of imaginative talent, in order to
produce an artist of the highest order. The special

tendency may lie in the direction of Painting, of Sculpture, of Architecture, of Music, or of any other Art for
the perfect expression of which imagination and science
are needful in an equal degree. In either case, its power
will be immeasurably augmented by combination with
mental qualities of exceptional brilliancy. And therefore it is that we constantly find great artists springing
from clever families not previously remarkable for the
cultivation of the particular form of Art to which they
have devoted themselves. There is nothing unnatural in
this. The fire of heaven-born genius shines with tenfold
brightness when united with hereditary clearness of
intellect: that is all. Over and over again this fortunate
concurrence of circumstances has led to the happiest
results ; but never to happier ones than in the case before
us.

The Mendelssohn family was an exceptionally talented
one. The branch of it with which we are now concerned, traces its origin from a Jewish schoolmaster of
Dessau, named Mendel ; a man of liberal education,
though, as a descendant of Abraham, deprived, by the
oppressive laws of the period at which he lived, of every
opportunity of acquiring knowledge, except by stealth.
On the 6th of September, 1729, the wife of this poor
but faithful representative of the chosen people gave
birth to a son, who was called Moses, and who in due
time became known in Dessau as Moses, the son of

Mendel—in German, Moses Mendels Sohn—whence the
origin of the family name. The child displayed a remarkable aptitude for learning; and, by the time he was
five years old, had advanced so far that his father decided upon placing him under the care of Rabbi Fränkel,
to whom he soon became devotedly attached, and with
whom he studied diligently. When Fränkel was summoned, some time afterwards, to occupy the post of chief
Rabbi at Berlin, Moses followed him to the capital on
foot; and, while supporting existence on a few pence
gained by copying, still managed to continue his studies,
in spite of poverty so grinding that his sole food consisted of a weekly loaf, on which he carefully marked
out his daily allowance, in order that he might not be
tempted by hunger to anticipate the morrow's meal.
Under every disadvantage that an unjust and cruel
legislature could throw in the way of a Jewish student,
the frugal youth rose, from this miserable beginning, to
a position in which he was universally recognised as the
most accomplished scholar in Europe. In 1763, he
married a maiden of his own Faith, named Fromet Gugen-
heim, the daughter of a Hamburg merchant. So rapa-
cious were the laws under which his people groaned that,
before he could obtain his marriage-licence, he was
compelled to spend a certain amount of money at the
royal Berlin china manufactory, without even being
permitted to choose the pieces he would buy. The

manager, having on hand twenty huge china apes, supposed to be unsaleable, insisted upon his choosing these;
and they are preserved in the family to this day as
priceless heirlooms.

Fromet bore Moses Mendelssohn three sons, named
Joseph, Abraham, and Nathan ; and three daughters,
Dorothea, Henrietta, and Recha; besides two other
children, one of whom died in infancy, and the other in
early boyhood. For the support of this large family
the now famous philosopher laboured incessantly, but
always with true scholarly reverence for a scholar's
work; dying on the 4th of January, 1786, and leaving
behind him a deathless fame, and three good sons, well
able to provide for the future needs of the family. Of
these, the eldest, Joseph, settled with his mother in
Hamburg ; where he succeeded in establishing a flourish-
ing banking-business. Abraham, born the 11th of December, 1776, and therefore ten years old at the time
of his father's death, was sent to Paris, whither his
sisters Dorothea and Henrietta soon afterwards followed
him. Dorothea was married, first, during her father's
lifetime, to a Jewish merchant, named Simon Veit, from
whom she was judicially separated in 1798 ; and afterwards, to the well-known writer, Friedrich von Schlegel.
Henrietta—the "Tante Jette" of the family correspondence—remained unmarried, and was, for many years,
governess to the daughter of General Sebastiani, so

fatally celebrated, at a later period, as the Duchesse de Praslin. Recha married a Mecklenburger, named Meyer, from whom, after a few years of domestic misery, she obtained a divorce. Dorothea and Henrietta became Roman Catholics in after-life, and derived lasting comfort from a change which they adopted from sincere conviction. Joseph and Nathan died, as they had lived, in the Jewish community; the one at the head of the family banking-establishment, the other in the enjoyment of a government appointment in Berlin. It is necessary that the reader should bear these details carefully in mind, for the descendants of Moses Mendelssohn were bound together by so devoted an *esprit de famille*, that it is impossible to separate the history of any one of them from that of the beloved relatives whose interests were too closely interwoven together to admit of even temporary isolation. For the present, it is true, we are chiefly concerned with the fortunes of the philosopher's second son; but it is none the less necessary that we should give a fair amount of attention to those of the collateral branches of the family.

CHAPTER II.

THE REMOVAL TO BERLIN.

OF Abraham Mendelssohn's career in Paris very little is known, except that, after working his way steadily upwards, he was fortunate enough, in 1803, to obtain the appointment of cashier in Messrs. Fould's banking-house. Resigning this post in 1804, he entered into partnership with his brother Joseph, in Hamburg; and, on the 26th of December in the same year, married Fräulein Leah Salomon, a Jewish lady, of considerable property, and quite exceptional accomplishments, residing at Berlin. The first fruit of this marriage was a daughter, named Fanny Cäcilie, born the 14th of November, 1805. The second was a son, Jakob Ludwig Felix, born, as we have already said, on the 3rd of February, 1809. Another daughter, Rebecka, followed on the 11th of April, 1811. Soon after the birth of this third child, Hamburg fell into the hands of the French, and the family, having incurred the displeasure of the invaders, were compelled to make their escape from the captured city by night, and take refuge in

Berlin, where the banking-business was carried on without interruption, though, after a time, Abraham withdrew from it, and opened another establishment on his own account. For some considerable time, the whole family lived together in a large house on the Neue Promenade, a retired street, with buildings on one side, and a canal bordered with trees on the other. Here, on the 30th of October, 1813, Abraham's youngest child, Paul, was born, ten days after the battle of Leipzig. And here the education of the children was continued, until Felix was sixteen years old, and Paul twelve.

And now it was Abraham's turn to take the step which his two elder sisters had already taken, with such comfort to themselves, and—so true, so loyal, was the bond of affection which cemented the whole family together—with the tacit consent, if not the inward approbation, of those of its members who still maintained the tenets of Judaism. Leah Salomon's elder brother had long been a Christian; and, in accordance with prevalent German custom, had, on his admission into the Lutheran community, assumed the surname of Bartholdy, in addition to his own. By his advice, Abraham decided to have his children baptized in accordance with the Lutheran formula, and educated as Protestant Christians. He seems to have adopted this course in the full conviction that he was doing the right thing for his children, though he had not, at first, the courage to take the same step himself. But this period of irresolution soon passed away, and no long time elapsed before he presented himself for baptism, at Frankfort, together with his faithful Leah, who took the two new Christian-names of Felicia and Paulina, in allusion to those of her two sons, while the whole family assumed the double surname by which its members have ever since been distinguished—that of Mendelssohn-Bartholdy.

The only relative from whom any opposition to this proceeding was apprehended was Leah's mother, Madame Salomon, who, in accordance with Israelitish custom, had solemnly cursed her son after his conversion to Christianity; but even she was eventually reconciled to the inevitable change, and, at the intercession of her granddaughter, Fanny, wrote to Salomon Bartholdy, to assure him of her forgiveness, "for Fanny's sake." The separation from the Jewish community was thenceforth complete; and, though the affection of the three brothers remained undiminished, the Mendelssohn-Bartholdys were everywhere recognised as a Christian family.

CHAPTER III.

FELIX'S CHILDHOOD.

ABRAHAM MENDELSSOHN was a man of firm character, and great general ability; and, though not himself an artist, was gifted with a far keener insight than most *dilettanti* into the higher qualities of art. With sufficient discernment to detect in his children the signs, not only of talent, but of innate genius, he was himself entirely destitute of imaginative power; and, in later life, he frankly confessed his inferior position between the more famous members of his house, in the well-known *bon-mot*, "Formerly I was the son of my father: I am now the father of my son."[1] But, if wanting in the qualities which made Moses Mendelssohn a philosopher, and Felix a musician, he was wise enough to exercise upon the education of the latter an influence which proved of infinite value to him in after-life. And in this he was nobly seconded by his wife, a woman of highly-cultured intellect, who devoted herself without reserve

[1] "*Früher war ich der Sohn meines Vaters : jetzt bin ich der Vater meines Sohnes.*"

to the education of her children, whom she governed with a gentle firmness which assured their life-long affection and reverence.

Leah Mendelssohn's accomplishments were both varied and comprehensive. She spoke French, English, and Italian fluently, was a good Greek scholar—though, with characteristic modesty, she read her Homer in strictest secrecy—played and sang with taste and judgment, and drew beautifully. The style of her pianoforte-playing may be fairly surmised from her remark, made soon after Fanny was born, that the child had "Bach-fugue fingers." After the flight of the family to Berlin, when Fanny was seven years old, and Felix three, she gave music-lessons to both the children, beginning with five minutes at a time, until they were able to keep their attention fixed for a longer period, and long after this she superintended their practice regularly, with excellent results.

In 1816, Abraham and Joseph Mendelssohn were summoned to Paris, on business connected with the indemnity demanded from France by Prussia, after the conclusion of the war. As Abraham took his family with him, this gave him the opportunity of placing the two elder children under the care of Madame Bigot, an excellent pianoforte-teacher, under whom they made great progress. On their return to Berlin, the care of their general education was committed to Heyse, the

father of the well-known novelist. Ludwig Berger also
gave them lessons in pianoforte-playing, and Zelter, in
Thorough-bass and Composition; Henning taught them
the Violin, and Rosel instructed them in drawing,
while Abraham and Leah superintended the entire process, keeping the little ones so closely to their work,
that, except on Sundays, they were expected to begin
their studies at five o'clock in the morning.

On the 24th of October, 1818, Felix first performed
in public, at a concert organized by Gugel, playing the
pianoforte part in a Trio by Woelfl. In the following
year he entered the Berlin Singakademie, as an Alto.
He now began to compose diligently, and some of his
childish works show a marvellous aptitude, both for construction, and the expression of definite musical ideas.
The earliest piece of which a dated autograph has
been preserved, is a Cantata, *In rührend feierlichen
Tönen,* finished January 13th, 1820. In that year he
also wrote a Pianoforte Trio, in three movements, two
Pianoforte Sonatas, four organ pieces, three Songs, a
Violin Sonata, a *Lustspiel* in three scenes, and other
pieces, comprising, altogether, nearly sixty distinct
movements. In 1821, he wrote two Operettas, *Die
beiden Pädagogen,* and *Soldatenliebschaft,* each in
one act; and part of a third, called *Die wandernden
Comödianten;* five Symphonies for stringed instruments,
nine Fugues, a set of Motets for four voices, and a

multitude of smaller pieces. The MSS. of these form
part of the great collection, in forty-four volumes, now
preserved in the Berlin Library, a priceless series
of records, showing the steady progress of his art-life,
from the period of its first awakening, in early childhood, to that of its full maturity and premature extinc-
tion in 1847. The music of all these pieces is carefully
written in the neat and regular hand so well known
to those who have had the privilege of examining his
scores. Nearly all are dated, and duly inscribed with
the name of the place at which they were composed;
and in many cases the pieces are headed with the
letters L.e.g.G. or H.d.m., which he constantly used to
the end of his life—hieroglyphics the interpretation of
which still remains a secret, even to his children, though
a guess has been hazarded to the effect that H.d.m.
may possibly mean *Hilf du mir* (Help Thou me).

It is rare, indeed, that so complete an index as this
to the life-work of a great artist is to be found in any
single collection. Perhaps the only instance of a similar one, equally complete, is the magnificent series of
Handel's autographs preserved in the Royal Library at
Buckingham Palace. By a singular coincidence, these
also are constantly distinguished at the end by three
letters—S.D.G.—which, however, are well known to
stand for *Soli Deo Gloria* (Glory to God alone).

In the spring of the year 1821 Carl Maria von

Weber visited Berlin, for the purpose of superintending
the production of *Der Freischütz* at the then newly-
erected German Opera-house; and Felix, naturally
attracted by the brilliancy of his genius and the beauty
of his greatest Opera, soon learned to regard him with an
admiration which he retained undiminished until the
end of his life. Sir Julius Benedict, in a lecture delivered
many years since, before the Camberwell Literary Institution, delighted his auditors with the story of his first
meeting, on this occasion, with the young composer,
who ran up to Weber in the street with a hearty and
affectionate greeting.

In the beginning of November, in the same year,
Zelter took Felix to Weimar, on a visit to Goethe, in
whose house he spent a happy fortnight. The poet received his youthful guest with undisguised affection;
and the letters written by Felix to his parents and
sisters contain an interesting description of the great
man's domestic life.

"We hurried downstairs," says Felix, in a letter dated Weimar,
November 6th, 1821, "and went to Goethe's house. He was in the
garden, just coming round a hedge. Is it not strange, dear
father—exactly as it happened with you? He is very kind; but
I do not think any of his portraits resemble him. He looked
through his interesting collection of fossils, which has been newly
arranged by his son, and said repeatedly, 'H'm! H'm! I am
quite satisfied.' After this I walked in the garden with him and
Professor Zelter for about half an hour. Then we went to dinner.
He does not look like a man of seventy-three, but rather of fifty.
After dinner, Fräulein Ulrike, Frau von Goethe's sister, asked him

for a kiss, and I followed her example. Every morning I have a kiss from the author of *Faust* and *Werther*, and every afternoon two kisses from father and friend Goethe. Think of that! In the afternoon I played to Goethe for about two hours, partly Fugues of Bach, and partly improvisations. In the evening they arranged a whist-table, and Professor Zelter, who took a hand, said, 'Whist means that you are to hold your tongue.' There is a good expression for you! We all had supper together; even Goethe, who does not generally take it."

In a second letter, dated November 10th, he writes :—

"On Thursday morning, the Grand Duke, the Duchess, and the Hereditary Grand Duke came to us, and I had to play. I played from eleven in the morning till ten in the evening, with only two hours' interruption, finishing with Hummel's Fantasia. When I was with him the other day, I played my Sonata in G minor, which he liked very much. . . . Every afternoon Goethe opens his instrument—a Streicher—with the words, I have not yet heard you to-day; now make a little noise for me.' And then he generally sits down by my side; and when I have done—mostly extemporising—I ask for a kiss, or take one. You cannot fancy how good and kind he is to me. It does not strike me that his figure is imposing. He is not much taller than father. But his look, his language, his name, they are imposing. The amount of sound in his voice is wonderful; he can shout like ten thousand warriors. . . . On Saturday evening, Adèle Schopenhauer was with us, and Goethe, contrary to his custom, spent the whole evening in our company. Our departure was mentioned, and Adèle proposed that we should all throw ourselves at Zelter's feet, and beg for a few days' delay. We dragged him into the room, and then Goethe began with his voice of thunder to abuse Zelter for wanting to take us to 'that old nest,' as he called it. He ordered him to be silent, and obey without resistance; to leave us here, go to Jena alone, and come back again. Professor Zelter was besieged on all sides, so he had to give in and do everything as Goethe wished. And now Goethe was assailed on all sides. They kissed his mouth, and his hands, and whoever could not get near them, patted and kissed his shoulders. If he had not been at home, I believe we should have carried him home in triumph. Fräulein Ulrike also embraced him. She is very pretty, and he makes love to her; so the whole thing had a fine effect. On Monday there was a concert at Frau von Henkel's. Of course, when Goethe says, 'There is company to-morrow at eleven, little one, and you too must play us something,' I cannot say 'No!'"

When Leah sent these letters to "Tante Jette," she wrote in reply, "If God spare him, his letters will, in long, long years to come, create the deepest interest. Take care of them as precious relics. They are sacred already, as the outpourings of a mind so pure and childlike." And she was right.

They are, indeed, marvellous effusions, combining a man's keen power of observation with the freshness of a child's enjoyment; overflowing with natural eloquence, yet bearing the stamp of literal truth on every sentence. Could the cleverest word-painter in Europe have produced a more delightful picture of Goethe in his moments of relaxation, than that which is here presented to us by a boy of twelve years old?

CHAPTER IV.

EARLY EFFORTS.

THAT great things should be expected from a child able thus easily to win the heart of a man so notoriously difficult of access as the author of *Faust* and *Wilhelm Meister*, is only natural. The wonder is that Felix should have passed unscathed through the temptations inseparable from a system of education which, notwithstanding the strictness of its discipline, addressed itself to the powers of a well-ordered intellect, at a period of life commonly supposed to be influenced solely by the instincts of childhood. Upon any ordinary boy, the effect of such a trial would have been disastrous. But, though Felix was accustomed to associate with men and women at an age when most parents would have confined him to the nursery; though he was treated with respect, rather than with indulgence, by the leaders of the German intellectual world, who, attracted by Abraham's good sense, and the irresistible charm of Leah's brilliant conversation, made the house in the Neue Promenade their favourite resort;

though his playing was praised, and his talent for improvisation openly and admiringly acknowledged; he is described, by all who knew him at this time, as the most natural and charming boy imaginable, utterly unspoiled by dangerous adulation, modest in manner, gentle in disposition, and withal rejoicing in health, and youth, and life, and the love of his devoted parents and sisters, and all that could make life worth living, and love its most precious possession.

Sir Julius Benedict tells us how, after working hard at his first Pianoforte Quartett in C minor (Op. 1), he " cleared high hedges with a leap," and " climbed up the trees like a squirrel."

Hiller describes him as springing up to Aloys Schmitt's shoulders, and making the good professor carry him along a narrow passage which led to the house in which he was staying. Devrient writes, " He took his place among grown people, in his child's dress, a tight-fitting jacket, cut very low at the neck, with full trousers buttoned over it. Into the slanting pockets of these, he loved to thrust his hands, rocking his head, covered with long brown curls, from side to side, and shifting restlessly from one foot to the other."

The curls were very remarkable. Hiller, Benedict, and all who remember Felix as a child, speak of them, and describe them as brown or auburn. In later life they became so dark that they might have been fairly called black.

Felix played in public, for the second time, on March 31st, 1822, at a concert given by Aloys Schmitt, with whom he played a Duet for two pianofortes, by Dussek. In the summer of that year, the whole family made a lengthened tour in Switzerland, stopping at Cassel, on their way to the frontier, for the purpose of introducing Felix to Spohr; and afterwards visiting, in turn, Schaffhausen, Lucerne, the St. Gotthard Pass, as far as Andermatt, Interlaken and the Wengern Alp, Berne, Vevey, and Chamouni. It will be readily understood that the children were not idle during their long holiday excursions, a fact which is sufficiently proved by the dated MSS. Felix wrote three Songs at Sécheron, near Geneva; and also began a second, and probably extensively altered, copy of the Pianoforte Quartett in C minor (Op. 1), at which Benedict had found him at work in the previous year.[1] On returning to Germany in the autumn, he paid a second visit to Goethe, at Weimar, and made the acquaintance of Schelble at Frankfurt.

On the 5th of December he played his Pianoforte Concerto in A minor, at a concert given by Frau Anna Milder; and during this year, and 1823, he wrote a multitude of pieces, including six Symphonies for stringed

---

[1] It is evident that this must have been a revised form of the work; for Benedict distinctly speaks of having seen Felix writing out the Quartett at Berlin, while the written date proves the finished copy to have been *begun* at Sécheron, September 18th, 1822.

instruments, five Concertos, a second Pianoforte Quartett in F minor (Op. 2), a Violin Sonata (Op. 4), a *Kyrie*
for two choirs, Psalm lxvi., a *Magnificat,* and a *Gloria*
with instrumental accompaniments, and an Opera in
three acts, entitled *Die beiden Neffen, oder der Onkel aus
Boston..*

Felix was now fourteen years old, growing rapidly,
and still more rapidly developing the intellectual
qualities which distinguished his character through life.
His hair was cut short; and his child's dress exchanged
for the usual boy's jacket and trousers of the period.
But his manners remained as natural and unaffected as
ever; and he still retained, in the loving home-circle,
the place which had been his since his earliest remembrance. His love for Fanny—returned, on her side, with
boundless confidence—was deep enough to influence the
lives of both, till the sad day when the sister's sudden
death broke the brother's heart. Leah used to say they
were " vain of one another;" and, though Rebecka and
Paul were so much younger, an intimate friendship sub-
sisted between them all.

The family still lived at No. 7 in the Neue Promenade,
and here, about this time, the children began to take
an active share in certain weekly performances of vocal
and instrumental music, which were given on Sunday
mornings in the large dining-room, with the assistance
of friendly artists, who rendered Felix's compositions

with true musician-like feeling, while he himself conducted the miniature Orchestra, standing upon a stool
that he might be the better seen—Fanny presiding at
the Pianoforte, Paul playing on the Violoncello, and
Rebecka taking part in the vocal music. The advantage of this wholesome practice was incalculable. Felix
was sure of hearing his music artistically interpreted;
and the prevailing tone of the performances was so
refined, that, as Sebastian Hensel tells us, "all musicians
of distinction passing through Berlin requested to be
admitted to the entertainments."

In 1823, Kalkbrenner constantly attended them; and
his candid criticisms were always gratefully received. On
February 3rd, 1824, Felix's fifteenth birthday, *Die beiden
Neffen* was rehearsed by the little association, for the
first time, with full Orchestra. At the supper which
followed, Felix's health was proposed, and Zelter, though
by nature as undemonstrative and morose as Cherubini
himself, took him by the hand, with the words, "From
this day, dear boy, thou art no longer an apprentice,
but an independent member of the brotherhood of
musicians. I proclaim thine independence, in the
names of Haydn, of Mozart, and of old Father Bach."

He then embraced the boy, and kissed him heartily;
and the rest of the evening was spent in toasts, and
merriment, and songs of triumph. The Opera was afterwards acted at home, with the unanimous approval of

the friends who were invited to see it; but no attempt was made to give it publicity, though its production in this form was an important advance upon the method of treatment observed with regard to *Die beiden Pädagogen*, and the other earlier dramatic works, which had only been sung without action.

Towards the close of this year, Moscheles paid a long visit to Berlin, and, as a matter of course, found ready admission to the inmost heart of the charmed circle. He was then thirty years of age. His reputation was already made; and he so delighted the Mendelssohns by his finished pianoforte-playing, that Abraham and Leah begged him to accept Felix as a pupil. This he declined to do. " He has no need of lessons," he writes in his diary; "if he sees anything noteworthy in my style of playing, he catches it from me at once." Nevertheless, he consented to give him his advice, and, in a later page of the diary, he writes, "To-day, from two to three, I gave Felix his first lesson; but not a moment could I conceal from myself the fact that I was with my master, not with my pupil." A week later he says, "He catches at the slightest hint I give, and guesses my meaning before I speak."

Spohr also visited Berlin in 1824, for the purpose of superintending the first performance in that city of his new Opera, *Jessonda*, and the intimacy begun at Cassel in 1822, was then renewed, with genuine pleasure on both sides. Great difficulties were thrown in the way of the new work, by Spontini; but its success was all that could be desired, and gave full satisfaction to the composer's friends.

Meanwhile, Felix made great advance in composition, producing during the course of this year, the Quartett in B minor (Op. 3), the Symphony in C minor (Op. 10), now known as No. I., but inscribed on the MS. belonging to the Philharmonic Society, No. XIII.; the Pianoforte Sestett (Op. 110, posth.), and other works, no longer to be criticised as exercises in composition, but as the productions of a matured artist. In none of these works do we find the slightest sign of haste, or carelessness, or that fatal craving for effect which ruins so many a youthful genius, more especially in cases exceptionally rich in opportunities of performance. Everything he wrote was conceived in an unvarying spirit of the truest reverence for Art, and always with a strict observance of its accepted canons.

In the spring of 1825, Abraham took his boy with him to Paris, where father and son were brought into daily intercourse with the best musicians then settled in the French capital. Rossini, Meyerbeer, Hummel, Onslow, Paer, Halévy, Kalkbrenner, Herz, Boucher, Rode, Baillot, Kreutzer, Pixis, and many more, rejoiced in doing honour to Felix's great talent; and even Cherubini, who rarely bestowed a word of praise or encourage-

ment on any one, treated him with unwonted consideration, recommending him to write a *Kyrie à cinq*, with
full Orchestra, which he afterwards described as the most
ambitious thing he had yet attempted. But his own
impression of the condition of music in Paris was anything but satisfactory. He complained of the want of
earnestness, the frivolous taste, the almost incredible
ignorance of great works known in Germany to every
one, the superficial aims of even the best masters with
whom he was brought into daily contact. With Auber
he was especially displeased; complaining bitterly of his
ignorance of the first principles of orchestral writing;
his miserable habit of confiding to the piccolo the office
of sustaining the chief interest of all his most prominent movements, one after the other; his persistent
blindness to the examples of instrumentation set before
him in the scores of Haydn, and Mozart, and Beethoven.
After his first experience of *Léocadie*, he sent a full
account of the opera to Fanny, telling her that "the
overture starts with a tremolando on the stringed instruments, and then the piccolo instantly begins on the
roof, and the bassoon in the cellar, and both blow away
at a melody. . . . The whole opera might be transcribed
for two flutes and a Jews' harp *ad libitum*." Fanny
resented this, and accused him of prejudice. But he insisted upon the point, and to the end of his life retained
his opinion unchanged. Cherubini was the only musician

in Paris whom he learned thoroughly to respect, not-withstanding the great man's repellent manner. He described him as "an extinct volcano, all covered with stones and ashes, yet now and then bursting into flame."

Abraham and Felix left Paris on the 19th of May, 1825, in company with Tante Jette, who thenceforth resided at Berlin, in the enjoyment of an ample pension paid to her by General Sebastiani, the education of whose daughter was by this time complete. On their way home, they paid a short visit to Goethe, who accepted with unconcealed pleasure the dedication of the Quartett in B minor; and during the remainder of the year Felix devoted himself with renewed energy to theoretical study, and technical practice, completing the well-known Capriccio in F sharp minor (Op. 5), and the "Trumpet Overture" (Op. 101, posth.); giving much time and thought to a more important dramatic work than any he had hitherto attempted, and producing an instru-mental piece which quite eclipsed the most successful of his earlier efforts.

The dramatic piece was *Die Hochzeit des Camacho*, an Opera, in two acts, the libretto for which, founded on an episode in the history of Don Quixote, had been prepared for him by his friend Klingemann. As we shall need to speak of this again, we will not stay to describe it now. The instrumental piece was the beautiful Ottetto for

Stringed Instruments (Op. 20). In freshness of conception, symmetrical proportion, and masterly treatment of a series of bold and well-considered subjects, this fine composition yields to few, if any, even of the most successful efforts of the master's later period; in poetical feeling, and the higher qualities of the imaginative school, it quite certainly yields to none. The leading idea of the scherzo—as he privately confessed to Fanny—was suggested by some lines in the scene of the *Walpurgis-Nacht*, from *Faust* :—

> Wolkenzug und Nebelflor
> Erhellen sich von oben;
> Luft im Laub, und Wind im Rohr,
> —Und alles ist zerstoben.

And the adaptation of the music to the poetical imagery is perfect.

The Capriccio is dated the 23rd of July, 1825. "Camacho's Wedding " was completed on the 10th of August; and the Ottetto, towards the close of October. Between these dates, an important family event took place.

As early as the month of February, 1825, Abraham Mendelssohn had meditated the purchase of a large family mansion, No. 3, Leipziger Strasse; and before the close of the year, he actually took possession of it. Here he and Leah lived to the end of their days; Fanny sharing it with them after her marriage, and retaining possession of a portion of it until her death. The rooms

were large and lofty, and one of them—Leah's boudoir
—opening by three arches into an adjoining apartment,
was admirably adapted for theatrical performances. The
house was surrounded by beautiful park-like grounds,
seven acres in extent, which, in the time of Frederick
the Great, had formed part of the *Thiergarten*. Here,
shaded by magnificent old trees, stood the now famous
Gartenhaus; afterwards occupied by Fanny and her
husband. The central portion of the building formed a
spacious hall, capable of comfortably seating several
hundred persons, and in this most convenient apartment,
the Sunday *matinées* were henceforth held. The whole
formed a delightful acquisition for the family, and but
for its damp situation, and incurable coldness, would
have been faultless. In summer it was simply perfect.[2]

In this new residence, a new life gradually developed
itself; or, rather, the old life ripened into fuller beauty,
as the children grew old enough to take their places in
the world, until, in process of time, the Mendelssohn-
Bartholdys learned to look upon the Leipziger Strasse
as part and parcel of their own existence—a kingdom
peopled with living types of their own peculiar tastes,
and feelings, and convictions, in which their dreams of

---

[2] After Felix's death, the property was sold to the government,
and the *Gartenhaus* was pulled down for the accommodation of
the Upper House of the Prussian Parliament. The street front
remains unchanged.

art and of philosophy were to be worked out with the happiest completeness, and from which unsympathising spirits were to be for ever hopelessly excluded. Sebastian Hensel tells us that the house was to them "no mere bricks and mortar, but a living individuality;" and this passionate identification of the family home with the family gifts and graces, is so constantly set forth in the family correspondence, that, without fully appreciating it, it would be impossible to penetrate to the inner life, either of Felix, or of those who were dearest to him.

CHAPTER V.

THE GARDEN HOUSE.

EVENTS soon proved that the influence exercised upon Felix's future by the new life in the Garden House was no superficial one. That it led to the first conception of the work upon which, more than upon any other, his fame will for ever mainly rest, is certain. It first made itself felt by the establishment of a more definite interchange of thought between the art-loving members of the community than had ever before existed. Pens, ink, and paper were laid out in one of the summer rooms, and each one wrote down the ideas that occurred to him as he wandered about the domain. The results were put together, from time to time, in the form of a *Garten-zeitung*. For this, in winter, was substituted a *Thee-und-Schneezeitung*, the contributions for which were placed in a tin box. Though the children were all good linguists, their knowledge of English was not yet sufficiently perfect to admit of the full appreciation of the beauties of Shakespeare in his own terse phrases. But about this time the clearness of the Schlegel-Tieck translation enabled them to read his poetry with

the fullest comprehension of its meaning that a para-
phrase could convey. Felix and Fanny were enchanted
with the beauties of the "Midsummer Night's Dream."
During the lovely summer months of 1826, they
naturally interchanged their ideas upon the subject,
through the medium of the *Gartenzeitung;* and thus it
was that Felix first conceived the delicious commentary
upon Shakespeare's faerie vision which would alone have
sufficed to make his name famous.

This lovely creation was first committed to paper in
the form of a pianoforte-piece *à quatre mains,* in which
condition Moscheles heard it, in 1826. "How great
was my delight," he writes, "when Felix played, with
his sister Fanny, his new *Overture to A Midsummer
Night's Dream !*" It must indeed have been a delight
to hear it so interpreted, while the composer himself
was revelling in the first freshness of his beautiful inspiration; but its presentation to Moscheles for the
first time in this simple form, is very suggestive, and
conveys a far deeper meaning than that which appears
upon the surface. The instrumentation of the piece
embodies effects so strikingly original, that it may fairly
be said to mark an æra, not only in Felix's art-life,
but in the history of orchestration itself, yet he did not
fear to entrust the interpretation of his inmost meaning,
in the first instance, to the limited capabilities of a single
instrument, and even to express his new thought through

this weak medium to a critic in whose opinion he placed unbounded confidence. And why? From first to last, from the starting-point of his career to the maturity of his bright art-life, he held the laws of colour to be wholly subservient to those of form. As Leonardo da Vinci and Raffaelle—nay, even Titian and Giorgione —*first* traced their designs on paper, with a bistre pen, or the end of a pointed crayon, and *afterwards* glorified them with the treasures of their palettes, so did Mendelssohn first rest, for the expression of his idea, upon the faultless proportions of its symmetrical form. When that was fully developed, and not till then, he proceeded to ornament his construction with the wonderful imagery which delights us to-day as much as it did those who first heard it fifty-seven years ago. And the principle involved in this process—the ornamentation of the construction, as opposed to the construction of the ornament—he never ceased to preach or to practise, to the end of his days. He regarded the canons of form laid down by Haydn, not merely as wholesome safeguards, but as elements indispensable to the stability of a firm and well-ordered design; and in later life he delighted in sketching out such designs, for the instruction of his pupils, in the simplest possible chords, and showing them how to clothe the skeleton thus formed with the graceful curves of a perfect and living body. That he himself was able to endow that body with a still more graceful and poetic soul, is a fact which this one work alone would sufficiently have proved, had he never written another. But, however wild or wayward the soul he imagined, he never strove to infuse it into a body of irregular construction ; and unless we bear this fact well in mind, we shall never truly understand his genius, nor learn to distinguish its peculiar bias from that of other great men who have chosen for themselves a different path.

The first orchestral performance of the Overture took place in the Garden House, towards the close of the year 1826, in the presence of a large company of delighted and astonished guests. The first public performance took place at Stettin, in February, 1827 Why that place was fixed upon as the scene of an event so significant, does not appear, but it is certain that Felix went thither to superintend its production ; and on his return a still more arduous task awaited him—the preparation for the stage of *Die Hochzeit des Camacho*.

We have spoken of the objections raised by Spontini, the then director of the Opera, to the production of Spohr's *Jessonda*, in 1824. Similar obstacles were now thrown in the way of Felix's maiden Opera, and though it was received with every appearance of enthusiasm when performed for the first time on the 29th of April, 1827, it never received a second representation. The real source of the intrigues which led to its suppression cannot now be ascertained. The illnesses of the performers were clearly pretended; and every one understood them to be so. Critics were merciless. Yet the work possessed real merits, and those of a high order, and showed much dramatic power. The most adverse reviewers, for instance, could not deny that the solemn passage of trombones which accompanied the entrance of the Knight of La Mancha was a master-stroke of dramatic power, and this was but a fair example of the general tone of the drama. Felix felt the injustice with which he had been treated very keenly; and some time elapsed before he was able to throw himself into his work again with his accustomed spirit. During the summer, he made an excursion with some friends into the Hartz Mountains, and described his adventures in some charming letters. This seemed to divert his mind for a time, and on his return he worked steadily, though his attention was not so far devoted to Art as to interfere with the general culture of his mind. In this year, he matriculated at the University of Berlin, forwarding for the occasion a translation, in German verse, of the *Andria* of Terence; and diligently following out the course of study prescribed by the *curriculum* of the college, yet still finding time for composition. Among the works produced before the end of the year, he completed his Quartett in A minor, a Motet—*Tu es Petrus*—with Orchestra, composed for

D

Fanny's birthday; and the splendid Prelude and Fugue in E minor (No. 1, Op. 35), which he wrote by the deathbed of his friend August Hanstein, whose hope in a blessed eternity he symbolised by the magnificent Chorale with which the work concludes.

The most important works produced during 1828, were a Cantata for the Tercentenary Festival of Albert Dürer, performed at the Singakademie ; a second Cantata, for a congress of science given under the presidency of A. von Humboldt; an *Antiphona* for four choirs, and the second Concert-Overture which takes its name from Goethe's *Meeresstille und Glückliche Fahrt*—a delightful inspiration, and full of rich poetic feeling, though scarcely on a level with its illustrious predecessor.

And now Felix devoted his energies with heart and soul to one of those great undertakings in which, with noble forgetfulness of self, he spared neither pain nor labour for the benefit of Art. The works of Sebastian Bach were as little known in Germany at that period, as they were years afterwards in England. Felix determined to make them known, and to that end organised a little choir of sixteen voices, for the practice of *The Passion according to S. Matthew.* He knew it all by heart, and accompanied it without the book. The scheme attracted a considerable amount of attention, and at last it was proposed that the work should be produced by the Singakademie, with a choir of between three and four hundred voices. To this, Zelter, the then director of the Akademie, offered an obstinate resistance ; but he yielded at last, though with the worst possible grace, and, on the 11th of March, 1829, the work was publicly performed for the first time since the death of its composer, Zelter refusing to help, and sitting among the audience. The success of the attempt was unbounded, and a second performance loudly demanded. Spontini did his best to prevent this, but the Crown Prince issued a command, and the work was again sung on the 21st of March, Bach's birthday. And thus began that great revival of the works of the grand old Kantor of the Thomas-Schule, which has steadily progressed until, both in Germany and in England, his name and music are familiar to all who make the slightest pretension to a taste for art.

The year 1829 was also signalised by another event, which exercised a lasting influence upon the family circle—the engagement of Fanny to Wilhelm Hensel, the well-known German painter. This good friend had been on terms of intimacy with the Mendelssohn-Bartholdys since 1821, and had long indulged in the hope of winning Fanny's affections. But Leah had forbidden any form of definite engagement, and even interdicted all correspondence between the young people, during the period of Hensel's residence in Rome, where he studied for five years, supported by a scholarship granted

to him by the Prussian Government. On his return to
Berlin, in October, 1828, this term of probation came to
an end, and on the 22nd of January, 1829, Fanny formally accepted his proposal, with the full consent of her
parents. Yet, still, there were difficulties in the way.
Great changes of feeling, and much development of
thought, had taken place during his long absence. He
was not a member of the charmed circle, which had a
manner and almost a language of its own. Felix did
not at first receive him very warmly; and he himself
was jealous of Fanny's affection for her brothers and
sisters, and longed to look upon her as exclusively his
own. All this, however, soon passed away. A portrait
which he painted of Felix gave them all a high idea of
his ability, and a humorous little sketch which he
called "The Wheel," in allusion to a name applied by
the initiated to the frequenters of the Garden House,
and the contributors to the *Gartenzeitung*, gained the
goodwill of the entire community, and made him free of
its secrets for life. Thenceforth all went smoothly, and
so completely was Hensel made one of the family, that
he contributed to its archives a series of portraits of
all the celebrities who, from time to time, were received
as its guests. So diligently did he devote himself to
this self-imposed and thoroughly congenial task, that
at the time of his death the collection filled forty-
seven volumes, and comprised upwards of a thousand

portraits, including, besides those of the family and its most intimate associates, faithful likenesses of C. M. von Weber, Paganini, Ernst, Hiller, Liszt, Clara Schumann, Gounod, Clara Novello, Lablache, Grisi, Pasta, Frau Milder, Frau Schröder-Devrient, Horace Vernet, Cornelius, Magnus, Kaulbach, Rauch, Thorwaldsen, Goethe, Heine, De la Motte Fouqué, Körner, Tieck, Hoffmann, Mrs. Austin, Bettina von Arnim, Hegel, Bunsen, Humboldt, Jacob Grimm, Lepsius, and hundreds of others ; all now in the safe keeping of his son Sebastian, and nearly all enriched with the autographs of the persons represented. It will be readily understood that such a work as this not only secured for him a place within the circumference of "The Wheel," but entitled him to the highest consideration of the exclusives of the Garden House. During the remainder of his life, he was as much a part of "No. 3, Leipziger Strasse," as Fanny herself.

CHAPTER VI.

THE FIRST VISIT TO ENGLAND.

FOR Felix also the year 1829 was a momentous one, for
it witnessed his first visit to England. He reached
London—" the grandest and most complicated monster
on the face of the earth "—on the 21st of April, and
during the greater part of his visit occupied apartments in Great Portland Street, at a house then known
as No. 103, but now as No. 79, at the corner of Riding-
house Street.

His visit was not a mere pleasure-excursion. Abraham
Mendelssohn had long hesitated as to the choice of a
career for his eldest son; and it was not until he had
well considered the matter, and asked advice of many a
friend in whose judgment he placed implicit confidence,
that he decided upon permitting him to devote himself
to music as a profession. Having once made up his
mind upon the subject, he treated it in earnest. There
was to be no drawing back. Felix must make up his
mind to live by his profession; and, in order that he
might have every opportunity for settling himself ad-

vantageously, it was decided that he should visit, by turns, some of the greatest and most promising capitals in Europe, and decide for himself the scene of his future labours. He began with London, and on the 25th of May, 1829, he made his first appearance before a London audience.

His *début* took place at a concert of the Philharmonic Society, then held in the Argyll Rooms; and the piece chosen was his first Symphony in C minor. François Cramer led him to the piano, "like a young lady," but he conducted in the usual manner with a *bâton*—a white one, which he had caused to be made on purpose. "The success," he says, "was beyond anything that I could ever have dreamed. I was received with immense applause. The adagio was encored; I preferred to bow my thanks and go on, for fear of wearying the audience; but the scherzo was so vigorously encored that I felt obliged to repeat it, and after the finale they continued applauding, while I was thanking the orchestra and shaking hands, and until I had left the room."

The next important event took place at the same rooms, on Saturday morning, the 30th of May, when he played Weber's *Concertstück* to a highly sympathetic audience, with immense applause. On the 24th of June, he directed the Overture to "A Midsummer Night's Dream," for the first time in this country, at a concert given by Drouet, the flute-player; and also played

Beethoven's Concerto in E flat, which had never before
been heard in England.   On returning home after this
concert, Mr. Attwood, the then organist of St. Paul's
Cathedral, left the score of the Overture in a hackney
coach; and, as it was never afterwards recovered, Felix
wrote out another from memory, without the variation of
a single note.   The Overture was again played on the
13th of July, at a concert given for a charitable purpose,
and on this occasion Felix played his Double Concerto in
E, for two pianofortes, with Moscheles.

Meanwhile, Felix was received into society with all
possible honour.   We hear of him at balls given by the
Duke of Devonshire, and the Marquess of Lansdowne;
at a state dinner of the Prussian Embassy; at the Opera,
and the House of Commons; at private parties, and all
manner of places of amusement.   His manners and
animation delighted every one, and he laid the foundation
of many firm friendships which proved of infinite value
to him during subsequent visits to this country.

After the close of the season, he started with Klingemann on a tour in Scotland, penetrating as far north as
the Island of Staffa, where he was inspired with the first
idea of the delightful Concert-Overture originally called
The Hebrides, but now better known as *Fingal's Cave*,
or the *Isles of Fingal.*   He gives the subject of this,
compressed into two staves, but with clear indications
of the intended instrumentation, in a letter dated, " On

one of the Hebrides, August 7th, 1829;" with the
remark, " In order to make you understand how extra-
ordinarily the Hebrides affected me, the following came
into my mind there." A little later, he spent some days
at the house of Mr. John Taylor, a relative of the late
Gresham Professor, at Coed-du, near Holywell, in North
Wales, where he wrote the three pianoforte pieces afterwards published as Op. 16. In a letter dated the 10th
of September, 1829, he calls them, " three of my best
piano compositions." The first, an Andante and Allegro
in A, was suggested by the perfume of some particularly
fine carnations, and headed, *Rosen und Nelken in Menge*
(Roses and carnations in plenty). The arpeggios, he
said, symbolised " the scent of the flowers rising up."
The second piece, known as *The Rivulet*, was suggested
by a real rivulet which flowed near the house. The third,
the little *Capriccio* in E minor, begins with a reiterated
B in alt, suggesting a passage played on the faerie
trumpets of the *Ecremocarpus*, a spray of which he drew
on the margin of the music paper.

On the 10th of September he returned to London,
taking apartments at No. 35, Bury Street, St. James's.
On the 17th he was thrown from a carriage, and hurt
his leg so severely that he was confined to bed for nearly
two months. Klingemann nursed him affectionately;
and Attwood, Hawes, and Sir Lewis and Lady Moller
did all that could be done to cheer him; but his dis-

appointment at his inevitable absence from Fanny's wedding, which took place on the 3rd of October, was bitter. However, by the first days of November he was once more in the Leipziger Strasse, though still unable to walk without a stick; and there he found Fanny Hensel and her husband, quietly settled for life, in the famous Garden House.

During the winter, he completed the "Reformation Symphony," for the Tercentary Festival of the Augsburg Confession; and, in conjunction with Klingemann, a *Liederspiel*, called *Heimkehr aus der Fremde* ("Son and Stranger"), performed on the 26th of December for his parents' silver wedding; together with several other pieces of importance. Though the intrigues connected with the production of *Camacho's Wedding*, and Bach's *Passion Music*, had made his position in Berlin very unpleasant, he was complimented, soon after his return, by the offer of a Professorship of Music in the University. This, however, he declined in favour of his friend Marx, and, on the 13th of May, 1830, he resumed the programme laid out for him by his father, and once more started on his experimental travels.

CHAPTER VII.

THE JOURNEY TO ITALY.

THIS second division of the long journeyings began with a delightful fortnight, spent at Weimar in closest intercourse with Goethe, from whom he parted, to meet no more, on the 3rd of June. The history of the visit is recorded in the first volume of the *Reisebriefe*, which, to be fully appreciated, must be read in full, and in the original German, for the English translation gives but a faint idea of the spirit which pervades the glowing pages.

From Weimar he proceeded to Munich, where he stayed a month, playing much, and making many friends. Passing thence through the Salzkammergut, he made his way by slow stages to Vienna, and there spent another month, no less brilliant than that he had passed at Munich. Early in September he left the Austrian capital, and, after pausing at Presburg to witness the coronation of the Crown Prince Ferdinand as King of Hungary, reached Venice on the 9th of October. Here he stayed but a short time. On the 22nd we find him at Florence, and, on the 1st of November, he settled for the winter in Rome, at Nro. 5, Piazza di Spagna.

He now set to work in earnest, devoting a certain number of hours every morning to study and composition; and in the afternoon visiting the Vatican, the Capitol, St. Peter's, the Borghese Gallery—everything that was most worthy of attention and study in the Eternal City— until by methodical arrangement, he had " made each day memorable," and impressed each object of interest indelibly upon his mind. His letters give a delightful account of the impressions he received while inspecting and diligently studying the various galleries and works of art which occupied so much of his time; and also of his visits to Santini and Baini, Donizetti and Benedict, Torlonia, and Bunsen, and Berlioz; to the Casa Bartholdy—the palazzo of his uncle Salomon Bartholdy, on the Monte Pincio—with its frescoes by Veit, Schadow, Cornelius, Overbeck, and Schnorr; and above all, to the Sistine Chapel, where, during the Holy Week of 1831, he heard the *Improperia* of Palestrina, and Allegri's *Miserere*, and the music which has made the Papal Choir famous from time immemorial. His remarks upon this are intensely interesting, and throw much light upon technical details previously shrouded in impenetrable mystery. But it is curious to observe, throughout, the effect of the Lutheran education, which completely blinded him to the intimate connexion of this wonderful music with the ritual for which alone it exists. For instance, in describing the method of singing the Psalms, he treats the recitation of long sentences on a single note—a practice familiar as the alphabet to the smallest English Chorister—as a special feature of the method peculiar to the Papal Choir, and abuses it roundly.

In April he spent some time in Naples, returning to Rome in June; and soon afterwards proceeding homewards, by Florence, Genoa, Milan, the Lago Maggiore, the Simplon, Martigny, Chamouni, Geneva, Grindewald, the Furka, Lucerne, and Engelberg; making a second and very important visit to Munich, where he composed, and, on the 17th of October, 1831, first performed his Pianoforte Concerto in G minor; and finally making his way by Stuttgart, Heidelberg, Frankfort, and Düsseldorf, to Paris, which he reached in the middle of December, and quitted in the following spring, to take up his residence in London for the second time, on the 23rd of April, 1832, at his old apartments, No. 103, Great Portland Street.

The compositions produced during the course of these protracted wanderings were neither few in number, nor of mean significance. His most serious undertaking was the musical illustration of Goethe's *Walpurgis-Nacht*, first conceived at Weimar, clothed in a certain amount of form and consistency in Rome, and finished, in its first state—very different from that in which we now know it

—at Milan. The first MS. is dated "Mailand, July 15, 1831." The so-called Scotch and Italian Symphonies were also begun in Rome, and well advanced before his return. The Fingal Overture in its first state —known as *Die Hebriden*—is dated Rome, December 16th, 1830. During his first visit to Munich, he composed an *Ave Maria* (Op. 23, No. 2), and a Cantata on *O Haupt voll Blut und Wunden ;* during the second, his *Pianoforte Concerto* in G minor. Those who are fortunate enough to remember his playing will not fail to recall with wonder the passage at bar 482 in which, after the orchestra had done its best to work up a grand *crescendo*, he took it out of their hands, and completed the climax with a single unaccompanied chord on the pianoforte, in such sort as to sum up the whole with the harmony which, in ordinary cases, would have been entrusted to the full force of the trumpets and drums. The result of the first production of the work, in company with the C minor Symphony, and the Overture to the "Midsummer Night's Dream," was so satisfactory that he was at once requested to compose an Opera for the Munich Theatre— a commission which he was so far inclined at the time to accept, that, at Düsseldorf, he held a serious consultation with Immermann, as to the possibility of founding a libretto on Shakespeare's "Tempest," though a fitting opportunity for carrying out the idea never arrived.

From Paris he wrote to his father, communicating

his determination, after all the experience he had gained during his travels, to settle in Germany; though he could not yet make up his mind as to the particular city best fitted for his permanent residence. With Paris he was no better pleased than during his former visit, notwithstanding the renewal of his pleasant intercourse with Hiller, and Baillot, and many other old friends, and a newer intimacy with Chopin, and Liszt. The Overture to the "Midsummer Night's Dream" was played at the Conservatoire, on the 19th of February, 1832; and the *Reformation Symphony* was rehearsed, but not accepted for performance. The *Ottetto* was performed at a solemn funeral service held in commemoration of Beethoven, and much more of his Church Music was played in private; but he was very much dissatisfied with the popular taste. His spirits were also much depressed by the death of his friend, Edward Ritz, on the 23rd of January, and of Goethe, on the 22nd of March, and the visit ended alarmingly with an attack of cholera.

In England, matters were very different. His old friends received him with delight. With the veteran glee-writer, Mr. W. Horsley, his sons Charles, and John, and his daughters, Miss Sophie Horsley (to whom he afterwards dedicated the fourth book of *Lieder ohne Worte*), and Mrs. Brunell, he formed a cordial and lasting friendship. His compositions and playing were more fully appreciated than ever. The "Hebrides" Overture was played at the Philharmonic Concert, on the 14th of May; on the 28th of May, and the 18th of June, he played his G minor Concerto. For Mori's Concert, he wrote the *Caprice Brillant in B* for Piano and Orchestra (Op. 22). On Sunday, the 10th of June, he played on the Organ at St. Paul's Cathedral, and excited so much attention by his treatment of the pedal-board, that a complete revolution in the style of English organ-playing may be dated from that memorable performance, though, at that time, the organ at St. Paul's was the only instrument in London with a C pedal-board, and therefore the only one on which Bach's music could be played without destructive changes. It was also during this visit that he published his first book of *Lieder ohne Worte*, at Novello's (then in Dean Street, Soho), and an arrangement of the Overture to "A Midsummer Night's Dream," *à quatre mains*, at Cramer's. Of the score of the "Hebrides," then unpublished, he presented a MS. copy to the Philharmonic Society, and the society presented him with a piece of plate. The only drawback to his pleasure was the news of the death of Zelter, which arrived while he was staying with Mr. Attwood, at Norwood. The professor passed away on the 15th of May, and Mendelssohn felt his loss severely; for the old man had taught him well, and in spite of his naturally severe disposition, treated him with unwonted kindness.

Mendelssohn returned to Berlin in July, 1832, and

found the garden-life materially unchanged, though his sister Rebecka had been married in May, to Professor Dirichlet. At the instance of his friend Devrient, he was nominated as a candidate for the office of director of the Singakadamie, vacant by the death of Zelter, but lost the election by sixty votes out of two hundred and thirty-six—a failure which annoyed him extremely, and rendered his position in Berlin even more uncomfortable than it had been since the failure of "Camacho's Wedding." Nevertheless he gave three concerts during the ensuing winter, playing, for the first time in Berlin, Beethoven's Pianoforte Concerto in G major, and producing his own *Walpurgis-Nacht*, *Reformation Symphony*, *Caprice* in B minor, and the three Concert Overtures, *A Midsummer Night's Dream*, *Die Hebriden*, and *Die Meeresstille*. On the 13th of March, 1833, he completed the *Italian Symphony* for the Philharmonic Society, and sent it to London with the *Trumpet Overture* and *Die Meeresstille*, in fulfilment of a commission for which the society had offered him a hundred pounds, on condition that the works were to remain their exclusive property for two years.[1] The Symphony was first performed on the 13th of May, 1833, and he made a third journey to London for the purpose of conducting it, taking possession of his old apartments in Great Portland

---

[1] The works asked for were : a symphony, an overture, and a vocal piece. The second overture was intended as a present.

Street, on the 26th of April. At the same concert he
played Mozart's Pianoforte Concerto in D minor, and at
one given by Moscheles, he played some variations *à
quatre mains* composed by the two friends conjointly. He
also stood godfather, during this visit, to Moscheles'
little son, then three months old.

Returning to Germany soon after the middle of May,
he proceeded at once to Düsseldorf, to make prepara-
tions for the approaching Lower Rhine Festival, which
he conducted, with immense success, on the 26th of
the same month ; the chief attractions being Handel's
Israel in Egypt, Beethoven's Overture to *Leonora*, and
Pastoral Symphony, and his own *Trumpet Overture*. So
great was the effect produced on this occasion by his
admirable discipline and management of the orchestra,
that he was at once offered the post of director of
all the public and private musical establishments of
the town, for a period of three years, with a salary
of six hundred thalers (corresponding to about eight or
nine hundred thalers at Berlin).[2] This appointment
Felix accepted without hesitation, and when all was
arranged he started off with his father for another
visit to London—his fourth—reaching Great Portland
Street on the 5th of June, and enjoying himself as much

---

[2] Six hundred thalers equal about £90 in English money.
The quotation is from a letter written by Abraham Mendelssohn,
who was present at th e Festival when the offer was made.

as ever. On the 10th of June, the *Trumpet Overt ure* was played at the Philharmonic. On the 23rd, he played on the organ at St. Paul's, Klingemann and others blowing the bellows. He also played much in private, enjoying himself thoroughly, as we learn from Abraham's letters, though he himself seems to have had no time for correspondence. On the 4th of August, the father and son returned home together, and on the 27th of September, the *Wanderjahre* came to an end, and Felix settled himself down for a time to the duties and cares of his new appointment at Düsseldorf.

CHAPTER VIII.

AT DÜSSELDORF.

THOUGH Mendelssohn's life at Düsseldorf was both busy and interesting, and abounding in opportunities for the exercise of the gifts he was so ready to devote to the service of Art, it was also beset with many serious difficulties.

The *quondam* director of the Church Music refused to listen to reason, and had to be superseded. He had allowed matters to lapse into so miserable a condition that there was not even any good music to be found; so Felix ransacked the libraries at Cologne, at Bonn, and Elberfeld, and brought back with him a large selection of Masses and Motets, by Palestrina and the great writers of the Italian School, for which at first the Düsseldorfers showed no very particular taste.

At the theatre matters were still more unsatisfactory. There had been a proposal for the foundation of a large and permanent theatre in the town, and Immermann had taken great interest in the preliminary arrangements. Mendelssohn threw himself heartily into the scheme; taking upon himself the management of the opera, and leaving that of the drama to Immermann.

He began by announcing a series of classical performances, the first of which was to be Mozart's *Don Juan,*
But the term "classical" gave great offence, which was
so much increased by an indispensable rise in the prices
for admission, that at the first performance a serious
disturbance took place, accompanied by such an uproar
that the curtain had to be lowered and raised again four
times before the middle of the first act. "I was about
to lay down my *bâton,*" says Felix, in a letter to his
father, "though I would very much rather have thrown
it at the heads of some of these fellows, when the uproar
suddenly subsided."

The second act then passed off quietly, and after the
curtain had fallen for the last time, a consultation was
held on the stage, "in a shower of fiery rain and gun-
powder smoke, among the black demons," as to the best
course to be pursued by the management. Felix declared he would not conduct again until a public apology
had been offered to himself and the performers. After
some days the leaders of the riot complied with this
condition, and the second performance was eminently
successful. *Don Juan* was followed by *Egmont,* with
Beethoven's music; and this by *Der Wasserträger (Les
deux Journées).* The performances were henceforth well
attended, and the scheme appeared to prosper. But
difficulties still continued to arise behind the scenes,
and these of so serious a nature that a fatal coldness

sprang up between Felix and Immermann. The former resigned the direction of the orchestra, and with it his salary; and, though he still consented to watch over the performances in his honorary capacity, all hope of the establishment of the Opera upon a firm and artistic basis seemed to have vanished. Still much valuable work was done, at concerts, and in other ways; and, upon the whole, the good predominated over the evil.

So far as Mendelssohn's own art-life was concerned, the most important event that took place during his stay at Düsseldorf was the first reduction to a tangible form of his long-cherished idea of writing an Oratorio for the Cäcilien-Verein at Frankfurt, on the subject of St. Paul. At this great work he laboured diligently, with satisfaction to his conscience, and every prospect of ultimate success. He himself arranged the text in conjunction with his friends Schubring and Bauer, and the Cäcilien-Verein looked forward with daily increasing interest to the privilege of performing the work under his own personal superintendence. When he conducted the Lower Rhine Festival, at Cologne, in 1835, he played the principal portions of the Oratorio to his father, mother, and sisters, who met him there in family conclave, and all were delighted with the result. The festival was no less successful than that which he had conducted at Düsseldorf. The chief works performed were Handel's *Solomon*, Beethoven's *Eighth Symphony*, and *Overture* (Op. 124), and a *Hymn*, and *March* by Cherubini. At the conclusion the committee presented Felix with a complete copy of Arnold's edition of Handel's works, in thirty-two volumes, handsomely bound in green. He felt this compliment deeply, and speaks with childlike simplicity, in his letters, of the pleasure he derived from the contemplation of the precious volumes.

Among the more important works produced by Felix during his residence at Düsseldorf, in addition to the half-completed *St. Paul,* were : the *Rondo* in E flat (Op. 29); the *Capriccios* in A minor and E (Op. 33. Nos. 1 and 2); the *Fugue* in A flat (Op. 35, No. 4); a large number of songs, including *Auf Flügeln des Gesänges;* the scena, *Infelice,* composed for the Philharmonic Society;[1] some *Lieder ohne Worte ;* and, better than all, the overture to *Die Schöne Melusine*—a delicious inspiration of the true Romantic School, second only in beauty to the Overture to " A Midsummer Night's Dream," and dated the 14th of November, 1833.

And now Felix was called upon to decide a question which, more than any other that had presented itself since his first entrance into active life, affected the whole of his future career. His engagement at Düsseldorf was to continue in force for three years. Before the second year had expired, he was invited to seek release from the appointment, in order that he might accept that of con-

[1] See footnote, page 49.

ductor of the famous Gewandhaus Concerts, at Leipzig. The invitation was conveyed to him through Herr Schleinitz, a distinguished amateur, and an influential member of the concert committee, who remained his faithful and devoted friend through all the vicissitudes of his later life. Not only was it couched in the most flattering terms, but it opened to him the highest and most honourable artistic position attainable in the German musical world. It was impossible that he could listen to such a proposal unmoved; but he would not accept it without first carefully considering its minutest bearings, both with regard to his own interests and the rights of others; and it was not until he had satisfied himself that he could fulfil the duties required of him with honour to himself, and without giving cause of offence or jealousy to brother artists, that he finally decided upon accepting the offer, and resigning his previous engagement in time to enable him to enter upon his new duties before the close of the year. The acceptance of the necessary resignation was obtained without difficulty; and after spending some time at Berlin with his father and mother, both of whom had suffered, since the festival at Cologne, from severe attacks of illness, he proceeded to Leipzig towards the close of August, and at once busied himself in making the necessary arrangements for beginning the season on the 4th of the forthcoming October.

CHAPTER IX.

AT THE GEWANDHAUS.

THE house first occupied by Mendelssohn in Leipzig, stood in Reichel's Garten, adjoining the Promenade; and so great was the delight with which he took possession of it, that he afterwards wrote, " When I first came to Leipzig, I thought I was in Paradise." Almost immediately after his arrival, he received a visit from Chopin, whom he took this opportunity of introducing to Fräulein Clara Wieck (afterwards Madame Schumann), then sixteen years old.

His next visitor was Moscheles, who stayed long enough to be present at several of the concerts. His old friend, Ferdinand David, was also of immense assistance to him in arranging the orchestra. It was natural that this gentleman's future should be bound up with his own; for both were born, within a year of one another, at the same house in Hamburg; and David was for some years a member of the orchestra at the Königstadt Theatre in Berlin. Mendelssohn now obtained for his friend the office of leader of the Gewandhaus

orchestra, with the title of Concertmeister, his own being
that of Kapellmeister, and the two worked together,
with true fraternal affection, until the bond of friendship
was severed by death.

The first concert of the season took place under
Mendelssohn's direction, on the 4th of October, 1835.
The first piece in the programme was the *Meeresstille* Overture; the last, Beethoven's Symphony No. IV,
in B flat. The Overture gave the greatest possible
delight, and the Symphony attracted much attention,
from the peculiar delicacy of the *nuances* which, under
the *bâton* of the new conductor, invested it with a
charm for which none of the frequenters of the concerts
were prepared. This Symphony was always a peculiar
favourite with Mendelssohn, and there were certain
passages in it which, as those familiar with his reading
cannot fail to remember, he delivered with a refinement
of feeling previously unknown. On the occasion re-
ferred to, this feeling was fully comprehended by the
habitués of the best concerts in Germany, and from
that time forward the bond established between Felix
and the musical world of Leipzig was connected by
ties which could never be broken.

At the second concert the principal piece was Mozart's
Symphony in E flat; at the fourth Mendelssohn played
his own *Concerto* in G minor; at the fifth, and sixth,
the symphonies were Haydn's No. 4, and Beethoven's

Eroica, all played to perfection, and received with intelligent enthusiasm. Mendelssohn's position in Leipzig was, therefore, firmly established, when, on the 14th of November, Rebecka Dirichlet passed through the town, and persuaded her brother and Moscheles to accompany her to Berlin for two days. This visit was a delightful one, and, but for a sad affliction which had befallen the beloved father of the family, would have given unalloyed pleasure to all its members.

Abraham Mendelssohn-Bartholdy had suffered for some time past from failing eyesight, and was now quite blind. Still, his health was good, and he enjoyed his son's visit exceedingly. All were very merry; and Felix returned to Leipzig with a light heart, in time for the next concert. How great, then, must have been the shock, when, on the morning of the 20th, Hensel, travelling post-haste from Berlin, brought him the sad news of his father's death! Abraham had been suffering from a slight cold, but no one supposed him to be really ill until the night of the 18th. Even at ten o'clock on the following morning, the doctor foresaw no danger. He then turned round in bed, saying that he would sleep a little—and half-an-hour afterwards his spirit passed away so gently that the watchers could not be sure of the moment of his departure. "It was the end of the righteous," writes Fanny, "a beautiful, enviable end, and I pray to God for a similar death, and will

strive through all my life to deserve it, as he deserved it." And we all know, now, that her prayer was
mercifully answered.

Felix started instantly for Berlin with Hensel, and
on the morning of Sunday, the 22nd, was by his
mother's side. After the first effect of the terrible blow
had so far passed away as to render calm thought
possible, he fell into a despondent mood and solitary
habits, which gave Fanny great uneasiness. But he
fell to work with energy, amounting almost to des-
peration; and because his father had taken great interest in *St. Paul*, and urged him to complete it, he at
once made it the great object of his life. His respon-
sibility for the excellence of the concerts was also very
grave, and cost him much anxious thought, though
all went well, and with a genial understanding between
himself and the Leipzigers, quite free from the petty
jealousies which had so cruelly vexed him in Berlin
and Düsseldorf.

This friendship between the town and the artist was
a source of lasting gratification to both, and tended
greatly to the interest of German Art; and from first
to last, no mean intrigue arose to weaken the feeling.
The Kapellmeister taught his audience, and finding
it both willing to learn, and able to comprehend the
lesson he made it the business of his life to teach, led
it, within the space of three short months, to the

crowning success of the season, Beethoven's great
Ninth Symphony, which was given on the 11th of
February, 1836, with an effect hitherto quite unknown
at the Gewandhaus.

Meanwhile *St. Paul* progressed so rapidly that by
the following spring it was ready for rehearsal. In
consequence of the alarming illness of Schelble, the
director of the Frankfurt Cäcilien-Verein, it was determined that the first performance should take place at
Düsseldorf, on the occasion of the Lower Rhine Festival.
The preliminary rehearsals for this were conducted by
Julius Rietz, and when Mendelssohn reached Düsseldorf,
in May, 1836, he found everything in readiness for his
superintendence. The festival began on the 22nd of
May, on which day *St. Paul* was sung for the first
time, with every desire on the part of the performers
to do it justice, and to the entire satisfaction of a
critical audience, on which it produced a profound
sensation. The present concert-room not being then in
existence, it was sung in the Rittersaal, which was far
too small for it, insomuch that Hiller describes the crash
of brass instruments between the phrases of the Chorale,
Wachet auf ("Sleepers, wake"), as "quite overpowering."
But there was no question concerning the success of
the work, though some of the early reviewers treated
it with patronizing condescension. Sterndale Bennett
—then twenty years old—Ferdinand Hiller, and David,

were all present at the performance. On the second day Mendelssohn and David played Beethoven's *Kreutzer Sonata*; and the programme of the festival included the *Ninth Symphony*, and two of the Overtures to *Leonora*, Mozart's *Davidde Penitente*, and one of Handel's *Chandos Anthems*.

After the festival, Mendelssohn agreed to take charge of the Frankfort Cäcilien-Verein for Schelble (who still continued seriously ill), until his duties once more recalled him to Leipzig. Frankfort was at this time especially dear to him. He had formed an intimate friendship with the family of Madame Jeanrenaud, (*née* Souchay), the widow of a pastor of the "French Reformed Church," who with her two daughters, Mesdemoiselles Julie and Cécile Charlotte Sophie, lived in a large house near the Fahrthor, on the Quay of the Main. To Mademoiselle Cécile, Felix soon became devotedly attached, though his manner was so diffident that the whole family at first looked upon Madame Jeanrenaud herself as the real source of attraction. It was, of course, impossible that this state of things should continue. But Felix had determined to examine his own heart thoroughly before making a definite proposal. When, therefore, after completing his engagement with the Cäcilien-Verein, he was ordered to Scheveningen, for a month's sea-bathing, he seized upon this opportunity of submitting his feelings to the test of separation, before deciding upon the most important step in his life. His affection survived the trial; and, satisfied that it would do so to the end, he made a formal proposal soon after his return, and on the 9th of September, 1836, wrote to his mother : " I can settle nothing till I have written to tell you that I have just been accepted by Cécile Jeanrenaud. My head is quite giddy from the events of the day, but I must write to you. I feel so rich and happy."

For three weeks Felix was left in uninterrupted enjoyment of Mademoiselle Jeanrenaud's society, but it was necessary that he should return to Leipzig in time for the concert season, which began in the first week of October. The first concert took place on the 2nd of the month. It opened with Beethoven's Overture to *Leonora*, No. 1—absolutely unknown until Mendelssohn introduced it at Düsseldorf—and ended with his Symphony in A, No. VII. At another concert, Sterndale Bennett made his first appearance at the Gewandhaus, in his own *Concerto* in C minor, which he played in his accustomed delicate manner to perfection. This piece, and his Overture to *The Naiads* completely won the Leipzig public, who, as Mendelssohn wrote to Fanny, "have all of a sudden become his friends and advisers. Indeed, he is the sole topic of conversation here now." On a later occasion, when the Finale to the second act of *Fidelio* formed part of the programme, the audience seized upon the words *Wer ein holdes Weib errungen* (He who has won a gentle wife), as peculiarly applicable to Felix's engagement, and succeeded, by their enthusiastic plaudits, in inducing him to extemporise upon the well-known melody. The concert season closed like that of the preceding year, with Beethoven's *Choral Symphony*. But beside the subscription series, Mendelssohn directed a performance of *Israel in Egypt* in the Paulus-Kirche, with a chorus of 250 voices, and a large orchestra, on the 7th of November, 1836; and on the 16th of March, 1837, *St. Paul* was sung in the same Church, with a multitude of changes introduced since the first performance at Düsseldorf, including additions and omissions, reducing it very nearly to the form in which we now know it in England.

With this first introduction of the new Oratorio to a Leipzig audience, the season closed; and immediately afterwards, Mendelssohn inaugurated his well-earned holiday by starting, without a moment's delay, for Frankfort.

CHAPTER X.

THE WEDDING.

WITH a clear conscience as to the work accomplished during the course of the winter, and an honorary degree of Doctor of Philosophy, conferred upon him by the University of Leipzig, Felix quitted the scene of his labours on the 17th of March, 1837, and on the 28th of the same month, the wedding took place at Frankfort, in the French Reformed Church, of which Madame Jeanrenaud's late husband had once been the pastor. On returning to the house by the Fahrthor, after the conclusion of the ceremony, the happy pair were greeted with a Bridal Chorus, composed expressly for the occasion by Ferdinand Hiller, and sung by a party of young ladies belonging to his private choral society. The performance was perfect, and the secret had been so well kept that both bride and bridegroom were deeply touched with the unexpected attention. The honeymoon was spent at Freiburg in Breisgau ; and after six weeks of uninterrupted enjoyment, Felix and his wife returned to

F

Frankfort, on a visit to Madame Jeanrenaud, on the 15th of May. The month of July they spent at Bingen —where Felix narrowly escaped drowning—Horcheim, Coblenz, and Düsseldorf. And on the 24th of August the happy husband was compelled to leave his young wife with her mother, in order that he might carry out an engagement to conduct *St. Paul* at the forthcoming Birmingham Festival.

He arrived in England, on his fifth visit, on the 27th, and on this occasion stayed with his friend Klinge-mann, at No. 4, Hobart Place, Eaton Square, where the two fellow-workers held some serious consultations as to the plan of a new Oratorio, in which the prominent figure was to be the Prophet Elijah. He had but little to do this year in London; but on Sunday, the 10th of September, he once more played on the organ at St. Paul's Cathedral; and on the following Tuesday he gave a particularly interesting performance at Christ Church, Newgate Street, on a large new instrument with a C pedal-board, which had been built under the direction of Dr. Gauntlett, by Messrs. Hill and Son, of London. Since his first performance in 1832, much attention had been given to the cultivation of true organ music in England, and also to the construction of English organs. Dr. Gauntlett laboured nobly in the cause of reform; and the interest he took in the subject is well shown in his critique on the performances of 1837, published in the *Musical World* for the 15th of September of that year.

On the evening of the 12th, Mendelssohn attended a performance of *St. Paul* by the Sacred Harmonic Society at Exeter Hall. He was forbidden to take an active part in this, by the terms of his engagement at Birmingham; but he spoke most enthusiastically of the "beautiful manner" in which the work was presented. On the following day he started for Birmingham, and on the 19th, the festival began. On the evening of that day, he extemporised on the magnificent new organ, on themes from Handel's *Solomon*, and Mozart's *Concerto* in D minor. On the 20th he conducted *St. Paul*, with immense applause. It had several times been performed in England already, first at Liverpool, on the 3rd of October, 1836, under the direction of Sir George Smart, and afterwards by the Sacred Harmonic Society; but its real popularity in this country dates from its first presentation under his own powerful *bâton*. On the 21st, he played his own new Pianoforte Concerto in D minor; and on the 22nd, Bach's Prelude and Fugue in E flat on "St. Anne's Tune." Immediately after this, he started on his return journey, passing through London without a pause, though he was met at the coach-office, at midnight, by a deputation from the Sacred Harmonic Society, who presented him with a silver snuff-box.

On the 27th of September, Felix rejoined Madame

Mendelssohn at Frankfurt, and on the 1st of October, he reached Leipzig, at two p.m., in time to conduct the first concert at the Gewandhaus on the same evening.

The house prepared for Madame Mendelssohn's reception was in Lurgenstein's Garden, by the Promenade. Neither Fanny nor Rebecka had as yet seen the beautiful young wife, and both seem to have felt hurt at this, though the circumstances which prevented their presence at the wedding were unavoidable. They corresponded with her, however, at considerable length, and not without playful allusions to the true state of their feelings. " I tell you candidly," Fanny says, in one of her letters, " when anybody comes to talk to me about your beauty and your eyes, it makes me quite cross. I have had enough of hearsay, and beautiful eyes were not made to be heard." That people should have talked about these things will scarcely surprise those who are familiar with the little portrait by Hensel, reproduced in *Die Familie Mendelssohn;* yet neither that charming sketch, nor the large picture by Magnus, gives anything like an adequate idea of the charm of expression and manner which once seen could never afterwards be forgotten. When the sisters really did meet, they formed no exception to the common rule, but yielded to the charm as readily as did all others who were brought within its influence, and thenceforth a true sisterly affection increased the happiness of the whole family.

Meanwhile the Gewandhaus Concerts prospered exceedingly, and Mendelssohn contributed many fine compositions to the *repertoire ;* among them the Forty-Second Psalm, the *Serenade,* and *Allegro giojoso* (Op. 43), the Quartett in B flat, and other pieces of equal interest. The concerts were also made memorable by the introduction and revival of many great works by other masters, such as Schubert's Symphony in C major, Beethoven's Violin Concerto, Gluck's Overture to *Iphigenia in Tauris,* a Quartett from Mozart's *Zaida,* a Finale from Méhul's *Uthal,* and other works designed to illustrate the progress of music in the series of "historical concerts."

In 1838 the principal singer was Miss Clara Novello ; in 1839, Mrs. Alfred Shaw ; while Mendelssohn's magnificent pianoforte-playing, and David's masterly performances on the violin, proved a never-failing attraction.

The idea of " Elijah " was also rapidly assuming form and consistency, though none of the music was as yet written. It was not without long and careful consideration that the earlier idea of adopting the history of St. Peter as the basis of the new work was abandoned ; but Mendelssohn seems to have been quite convinced at last that that of Elijah offered fairer opportunities for musical treatment, and, his mind once made up, he never afterwards hesitated as to his plan of action.

In 1838 he conducted the Lower Rhine Festival at

Cologne, introducing an entire Choral Cantata by Bach —an unheard-of innovation at that time. In 1839, he wrote the Overture to *Ruy Blas,* for the Leipzig Theatre, and set to music the 114th Psalm. In the same year, he conducted the Lower Rhine Festival at Düsseldorf, the programme for which included Handel's *Messiah,* Beethoven's *Eroica* Symphony, and Mass in C, and his own Forty-Second Psalm. This work accomplished, he proceeded to Frankfurt, on a visit to Madame Jeanrenaud,. whose eldest daughter was married this year to Herr Julius Schunck of Leipzig.

Among the new works produced during the concert season of 1839—1840, were : the Pianoforte Trio in D minor, the hymn *Verleih uns Frieden,* and the 114th Psalm. The Ottetto was also given with great effect, the two viola parts being played by Mendelssohn and Kalliwoda. At one of the concerts Beethoven's four Overtures to *Leonora* and *Fidelio,* though not included in the programme, were presented at different times during the evening, by a happy inspiration with which Mendelssohn was visited during the time of performance. Nowhere but at the Gewandhaus, and under no other conductor than Mendelssohn, could such an idea have been so happily improvised, or so successfully carried out. But there the delight of the audience, who were always thoroughly *en rapport* with their beloved Kapellmeister, was unbounded. During the course of the season

Schubert's Symphony No. 9, was played three times—an unheard-of incident in the history of the concerts. A *soirée* was given by Mendelssohn, at the Gewandhaus, in honour of Liszt, who visited Leipzig in April, 1840, and between whom and the public there had arisen a coldness which this genial *réunion* happily removed. Ernst also appeared at one of the concerts, and, on April the 2nd, Hiller's oratorio, "Jeremiah," was played with great success.

But the year 1840 was rendered memorable by two events of far greater importance than any to which we have here alluded.

On the 24th and 25th of June, a festival was held in Leipzig, to celebrate the invention of printing. For this Mendelssohn composed a *Festgesang* for men's voices, and his famous *Lobgesang*. The former, not published until after his death, is best known in England by a Volkslied, tortured into connexion with the words of a grand old Christmas carol. The last is undoubtedly one of the master's greatest works. From first to last it breathes a spirit of exultant praise which we do not find surpassed in any part of his two great Oratorios. The treatment of the prevailing theme—identical, so far as its intervals are concerned, with the intonation of the Eighth Gregorian Psalm-tone—is masterly in the extreme. The wealth of melody which pervades the solo portions of the work is inexhaustible. And the expression of the whole, founded evidently upon the results of deep and earnest thought, is faultless. As one example out of many, it is only necessary to refer to the lovely tenor Arioso, *He healeth all your sorrows*, in which the wailing intervals of the minor mode are used with such consummate skill that, notwithstanding the reality and even the sweetness of the healing power, one can never for a moment forget the immensity of the sorrow it is sent to alleviate.

The other important event which took place in the year 1840 was a proposal, made by Mendelssohn to the Saxon Government, for the establishment in Leipzig of a national *Conservatorium der Musik.* A large legacy had been left to the town by a certain Herr von Blümner, and this he endeavoured to secure, and eventually succeeded in securing, for the above-mentioned purpose. As we shall have to speak of this project again, we will not pause to discuss it in detail now, but will content ourselves with saying that the preliminary steps were judiciously taken, and that the management of the scheme offered a striking contrast to the official blunders which completely paralyzed a similar undertaking, proposed almost simultaneously, by the King of Prussia at Berlin.

Finally, it was in this eventful year that Mendelssohn first entertained the idea of erecting a monument in front of the *Thomas-Schule* at Leipzig, in memory of Johann

Sebastian Bach, who had held the office of Kantor in the time-honoured college, and died within its precincts, on the 28th' of July, 1750. For this purpose he gave a number of concerts, for one of which—an organ recital in the Thomas-Kirche—he practised so much that he told his mother " the mere walking along the streets was like playing a pedal-passage."

CHAPTER XI.

IN LONDON AND LEIPZIG.

THE fame of the *Lobgesang* spread far and wide, reaching England so soon that, even before the first performance in Leipzig, Mr. Moore, who was then the life and soul of music in Birmingham, proposed to secure it for the festival which was to take place there in September, 1840. To this arrangement Mendelssohn gladly consented. The work was accordingly rehearsed in the Hanover Square Rooms, under the direction of Moscheles and Knyvett, Mr. Turle presiding at the organ. On the 18th of the month, Mendelssohn arrived in London for for the sixth time, and again became the guest of Klingemann. At this gentleman's house in Hobart Place he remained until the 20th, on which day he proceeded with Moscheles to Birmingham, where he accepted the hospitality of Mr. Moore. All was now ready for the approaching performance, which began on Tuesday, the 22nd of September. At the first concert, he played a Fugue on the Organ. The *Lobgesang* was sung on the 23rd, and received with acclamations. After this day's performance, he played on the organ for nearly an hour in private; and, at the evening concert, he played his Pianoforte Concerto in G minor. On the 24th, he gave an extempore performance on the organ, on themes from Handel's *Jephtha*. On the 30th he was again in London, where, surrounded by his friends the Horsleys, Klingemann, Moscheles, and other kindred spirits, he played on a fine organ, with C pedal-board, designed by Dr. Gauntlett, and lately erected by Messrs. Hill and Sons at St. Peter's, Cornhill. It was now time that he should return to Leipzig, without a moment's delay. He was already too late for the first concert; but, accompanied by Moscheles and Chorley, he arrived in time for the second; and, a few days after this, he gave a *soirée*, at the Gewandhaus, in honour of his friends' visit, on which occasion Bach's Triple Pianoforte Concerto was played by Madame Clara Schumann, Moscheles, and himself. We may well doubt whether, before or since, that great work has ever been interpreted by three such accomplished artists, or with such a perfect appreciation of the composer's intention.

By special command of the King of Saxony, the *Lobgesang* was twice performed at the Gewandhaus during the course of the season. It never failed to touch the hearts of all who heard it, yet Mendelssohn himself was far from satisfied with his own work, and made so many changes, while preparing it for these important performances, that it became necessary to destroy the plates engraved for Birmingham, and reproduce the whole, which now, for the first time, included the striking tenor Solo and Chorus, *Watchman! will the night soon pass?*—a scene which, as he himself told Herr Schleinitz, suggested itself to him during a sleepless night in Leipzig. So great was the effect produced at the second performance, in December, that, at the conclusion of the concert, the King rose from his seat, and walked straight up to the orchestra, where, in the kindest and most gracious manner, he thanked the composer and performers for the pleasure they had given him. It was a good augury for the future of Mendelssohn's schemes for the cultivation of music in Leipzig, and especially for that which was daily becoming more dear to his heart—the foundation of the Conservatorium.

CHAPTER XII.

DIFFICULTIES AT BERLIN.

A GREATER contrast than that presented by the honest and intelligent appreciation of Mendelssohn's work in Leipzig, and the miserable intrigues and jealousies which hindered its progress in Berlin, it would be difficult to imagine.

King Friedrich Wilhelm IV, on whom the crown of Prussia devolved on the 7th of June, 1840, was anxious to signalise his accession by the foundation of a National Academy of Arts, expressly intended for the cultivation of Painting, Sculpture, Architecture, and Music; each department being placed under a director of its own, and each director being invested, in his turn, with the superintendence of the whole academy. The control of the musical department was at once offered to Mendelssohn, with a stipend of 3000 thalers per annum, equal to about 450*l.* in English money. The scheme, as drawn up upon paper, was a tempting one; but Mendelssohn foresaw immense difficulties in the way of putting it into practice, and would willingly have declined the proferred honour, had it been possible to do so without disloyalty. But this it was not. The King pressed the appointment upon him ; and he had no choice but to accept. It must be confessed that the duties connected with it were sufficiently onerous ; including the foundation of a Conservatorium on an extensive scale, and the arrangement of concerts, in which the students were to take part in conjunction with *virtuosi* from the Court Theatre. He himself was to receive the title of Kapellmeister to the King of Prussia; that of Kapellmeister to the King of Saxony having already been conferred upon him at Leipzig ; and King Friedrich Wilhelm seems, from the first, to have been really anxious to do him honour—so much so, that, but for court intrigues and official blunders, a great work might undoubtedly have been accomplished. He himself hoped earnestly that this might be the case ; and, accepting the appointment experimentally for a year, he once more took up his residence in the Leipziger Strasse, entrusted the provisional direction of the Gewandhaus Concerts to Ferdinand David, gave his undivided attention to the work set before him, and in due time submitted his proposals for the future to the Prussian Government.

The result was a succession of petty vexations and annoyances which soon proved the main features of the scheme to be impracticable. Still, it led to the production of some works which the world could ill afford

to lose. Among others, to the presentation upon the
German stage of the *Antigone* of Sophocles, prepared a
the King's suggestion by Tieck, translated from the
Greek by Donner, and illustrated with choruses, entr'actes
and other necessary music, by Mendelssohn. This
great work was first performed at the Neue Palast
at Potsdam, on the 28th of October, 1841, and produced
a profound impression upon the cultivated few who were
able to appreciate the composer's intention, and the
skill with which it was carried out.

The task suggested by the King's taste for classical
literature was no light one. Its chief difficulty lay in
the selection of a fitting form of treatment. We know
absolutely nothing of the musical praxis of the early
Greeks. The endeavour to illustrate their sombre
tragedy, by aid of the polyphonic progressions of the
16th century would have been as great a mistake as
the introduction of the lighter forms of modern Italian
melody—perhaps, even a greater one; for we are
certain that the Greeks knew nothing of counterpoint, though it would be unreasonable to suppose
that they were insensible to the charms of instinctive
national song. What their national songs were, we
cannot even guess. But the human heart is the same
in all ages. Mendelssohn, therefore, adopted the only
reasonable course, by expressing the emotions set forth
in the tragedy in the form of musical language most

familiar to himself. The only point in which he has departed from his usual custom was the free use of the harp in the accompaniment of the chorus—an arrangement which, though it seriously impaired—as it always does—the rich tone of the modern orchestra, added greatly to the truth of the classical picture, by supplying the place of the lyre and other instruments of the extinct *testudo* family.

Though overwhelmed with work, much of which was of anything but a congenial nature, Mendelssohn still found time to pay a few brief visits to his beloved Leipzig, where he was always happy, and always sure of an affectionate welcome. On one of these occasions he played Beethoven's Pianoforte Concerto in C major, then quite unknown in Leipzig. On another he directed for the first time his own Scotch Symphony—No. 3, in A minor. It will be remembered that he began this at Rome, in 1831. The complete MS., dated the 20th of June, 1842, received its last touches at Berlin. In none of his great instrumental works is he more completely himself than in this. The Highland character of the opening Allegro and Scherzo, unmistakable as it is, falls everywhere into the rhythmic swing of the composer's favourite method of phrasing, without for a moment ceasing to breathe of the hills, and the heather, and the thousand Celtic surroundings which make its name so strikingly appropriate. And even the rich instru-

mentation, with its gorgeous and varied colouring, serves
only to bring the Caledonian simplicity of the leading
melodies into more prominent relief in passages in which
one might not unnaturally have feared that it would
tend to overload it. The first performance took place on
the 13th of March, 1842 ; the second a week later, after his
return to Berlin. In May, he once more undertook the
direction of the festival at Düsseldorf. This came to a
close on the 17th, and immediately afterwards he proceeded with Madame Mendelssohn to London, for the
purpose of conducting the new Symphony at the Philharmonic Concert.

The events of this his seventh visit to this country
were very important. The Symphony, played on the
13th of June, was received with acclamation. On the
27th, he played his Second Concerto in D minor; and
conducted the *Hebriden* Overture, now called *The Isles of
Fingal*. He played on the organ at St. Peter's, Cornhill, and Christ Church, Newgate Street. On the former
occasion—Sunday, the 12th of June—the congregation
had been singing a Hymn to Haydn's well-known tune,
Gott erhalte Franz den Kaiser, and on this theme he extemporised the concluding voluntary. At Christ Church,
four days afterwards, he again treated the same theme,
but in a wholly different manner, terminating with a long
and elaborately-developed Fugue. During the course of
the Fantasia by which this Fugue was introduced, a long

G

treble A 'began to sound on the swell. Mendelssohn
accompanied it in the form of an inverted organ-point of
prodigious length, treating it with the most ingenious and
delightful harmonies, his invention of which seemed to be
inexhaustible. We were very young in those days; but
we well remember whispering to our kind old friend,
Mr. Vincent Novello, who was sitting next to us at the
east end of the Church : " It must be a cypher;" and
he quite agreed with us. After harmonising the note
in an infinity of different ways, with ever-varying
passages which would probably have filled some pages
of music-paper, he at last confirmed our impression by
leaving it to sound, for some considerable time, alone.
By this time, all present were convinced that, during
the remainder of the performance, that particular
manual would be useless ; when to our astonishment,
the A quietly glided through G sharp and G natural to
F sharp ; and the organ-point came to the most natural
conclusion imaginable. While he was amusing himself with this little *plaisanterie,* a number of in-
considerate persons had the bad taste to crowd so
closely round the unusually confined and inconvenient
organ-loft, that, to save himself from fainting, Mendelssohn was compelled to leave off in the middle of an
unfinished passage, and make his way to the staircase.
He was so ghastly pale, that it was feared he really
would faint, but after breathing the fresh air, he speedily

revived, and as he passed down the stairs, he laughed and said, "You thought it was a cypher, I know you did."

It was during this week that the author of the present memoir first enjoyed the privilege of a personal introduction to the *Maestro* to whom he owes more than he can ever find words to express. The circumstances were these : We had been reading Cherubini one morning, with a dear old friend[1] who possessed a valuable musical library, to which no earnest student was ever denied access ; when a question arose as to the treatment of a certain form of counterpoint by Sebastian Bach. "If you will look on such and such a shelf," said our friend, who was totally blind, "you will find a MS. copy of ' the XLVIII.,' and you can then look out some passages." We set up the loose sheets on the desk of a beautiful old clavichord, the gem of our friend's collection, and asked for the history of the MS., which was a very curious one. "I bought it at a sale," said our friend, "and have always believed it to be a genuine autograph. I have a great mind to ask Mendelssohn about it. What do you say to calling upon him this morning, and taking our chance of finding him at home ?" This was a chance indeed ! Without the loss of a minute we started on our way to Denmark Hill, where Mendelssohn was staying at the house of Mr. Benecke,

[1] Mr. J. G. Emmett.

Madame Mendelssohn's cousin. We found him at home,
and were received with the kindest welcome. He knew
our old friend well, took the greatest interest in the
MS., and pronounced it genuine without a moment's
hesitation. Noticing the eagerness with which we
listened to his remarks upon the peculiarities of the
handwriting, he made us sit down by his side, and
pointed out everything that was noteworthy, with as
much attention to detail as if he had been giving a
lecture. Then he passed on to other subjects, asked us
about our own plans for study, and spoke so warmly of
Leipzig that, from that time forward, a visit to the
Gewandhaus became the dream of our life.

CHAPTER XIII.

AT BUCKINGHAM PALACE.

MENDELSSOHN remained a month in London, and during that time was honoured by her Majesty with two invitations to Buckingham Palace, where he was treated with marked consideration, both by the Queen and the Prince Consort. The details of the several visits are charmingly described in a letter dated July 19th, 1824, and addressed to his mother—perhaps the best known, and certainly not the least interesting, letter to be found in the whole cycle of his correspondence. He here tells us how the Prince Consort played a Chorale upon the organ by heart, and with the pedals, and so charmingly, and clearly, and correctly, that it would have done credit to any professor; and how, when he himself played "How lovely are the messengers," the Queen and the Prince both began to sing, while the latter changed the stops "so cleverly that I was really enchanted;" how he accompanied the Queen in *"Schöner und schöner,"* supposed to be his own, but really composed by Fanny, and afterwards in the *Pilgerspruch*, really his own,

both of which her Majesty sang "quite faultlessly,
and with charming feeling and expression;" how the
Queen picked up some music that had blown about the
room ; how he had to carry out the parrot, cage and all,
to prevent it from drowning the music with its screams ;
and finally, how the Prince Consort presented him, in
the Queen's name, with "a beautiful ring, on which is
engraved V.R. 1842;" and how her Majesty accepted
the proffered dedication of the "Scotch Symphony."

On the 10th of July, Mendelssohn and his wife returned to Germany. The month of August was spent
in Switzerland, and part of September at Frankfort.
The first Gewandhaus Concert for the winter season of
1842 took place on the 2nd of October, and this
Mendelssohn was able to conduct in person. He then
proceeded to Berlin, where he found everything in so
unsatisfactory a condition that he felt he had no choice
but to tender his resignation. The King did not absolutely refuse to accept this, but he made new proposals
which it was impossible to resist, and the result of these
was that Mendelssohn was installed as General-Music-
Direktor, with command of a small choir and orchestra
for church music on Sundays and festivals, and a salary
of 1500 thalers. The King hoped this select band and
chorus would serve as a nucleus for a greater one, and
while this was in course of formation Mendelssohn had
free permission to live where he pleased.

Mendelssohn now returned to Leipzig, where he busied himself in preparing the first composition required of him by the King of Prussia, under the terms of the new bond, viz. the music for *Œdipus Coloneus*, Racine's *Athalie*, and Shakespeare's *Tempest*, and *Midsummer Night's Dream*. The labour involved in the simultaneous preparation of so many different works, each with a distinct character of its own, was excessive; but he fell to with a will, and the year would have been a very happy one, but that the Angel of Death was again busy in the house he loved so well.

There had been a family gathering in the Leipziger Strasse, on Sunday, the 11th of December, 1842; and late in the evening, in the midst of a lively conversation, Leah Mendelssohn-Bartholdy was suddenly taken ill, and had to be carried to bed. She soon fell asleep, in her customary position, and remained to all appearance perfectly comfortable, until half-past nine on Monday morning, December 12th, when her gentle spirit passed away. There was no time to communicate with Felix until all was over.

He felt the blow severely, and was haunted by a fear that the family bond might be weakened now that the head was gone. But it was too close for that. The brothers and sisters remained as deeply attached as ever, though the loss of such a mother was a bitter trial to them all.

CHAPTER XIV.

CONCERNING THE CONSERVATORIUM.

THE year 1843 was an eventful one in its relation to the progress of Art.

It witnessed in Leipzig the realisation of Mendelssohn's long-cherished idea—the establishment of the *Conservatorium der Musik*. The King of Saxony, after duly considering the proposals laid before him, decided upon endowing the infant college with the legacy bequeathed by Herr Blümner. The funds thus placed at the disposal of the directors, though not inexhaustible, sufficed to start the institution on a firm though modest basis, and on the 16th of January a prospectus was issued, for the purpose of acquainting the public with the details of the proposed scheme. The first professors were: for composition and the pianoforte, Mendelssohn and Schumann ; for harmony and counterpoint, Hauptmann—the most learned contrapuntist in Europe, and the then representative of Sebastian Bach, as Kantor of the Thomas-Schule ; for the violin and management of the orchestra, Ferdinand David; for the organ, Fr. Becker; and for singing, Herr Pohlenz. Classes were also provided for the study of the Italian language, and the history of music. Pohlenz died before the opening of the college, and the management of his classes was confided to Madame Bünau Grabau, and Herr Böhme. The names of intending students were received on the 23rd of March. Of forty-six applicants forty-two were accepted. A portion of the Gewandhaus was granted for the temporary accommodation of the classes, and, on the 3rd of April, the Conservatorium was formally opened in the King's name, by the minister Von Falkenstein. A worthy pendant to the inauguration of the Conservatorium was the unveiling of the statue of Sebastian Bach on the 23rd of April. The ceremony was preceded by a concert, consisting entirely of compositions by the immortal fuguist; and the interest of the proceedings was not a little increased by the presence of one of his grandsons—a veteran Kapellmeister, eighty-three years old.

Meanwhile the busy pen was more busily at work than ever. *Elijah* was already beginning to occupy the foremost place in the composer's mind, though none of the music was as yet committed to paper. The King of Prussia was also impatiently awaiting the important compositions he had commissioned Mendelssohn to prepare for Berlin; and one of these, the *Incidental Music for the* " *Midsummer Night's Dream,*" was produced in the New Palace at Potsdam, on the 24th of October. The reception of this now famous music was enthusiastic; though so little were the beauties of Shakespeare's delightful drama appreciated in the Prussian capital, that an old *habitué* of the court, who sat next to Mendelssohn at supper, said to him: " What a pity that you wasted your beautiful music on so stupid a play." Happily for the interests of Art, the " stupid play " was not permitted to suffer from want of efficient representation. Immense care was bestowed upon the scenery and dresses; and the entire performance, the details of which were superintended by Tieck on the stage, and Mendelssohn in the orchestra, was irreproachable. The perfect adaptation of the music to the situations of the drama was recognised by all who were capable of forming an independent opinion on the subject, and in a letter dated the 18th of October, 1843, Madame Hensel describes the events of the evening to her sister Rebecka, in terms which leave no room for doubt as to its triumphant success.[1]

With so much hard work provided for him by the King of Prussia, it was clear that, notwithstanding the stipulation which left him free to make himself a home wherever he pleased, Mendelssohn could no longer continue to reside permanently in Leipzig. Accordingly

[1] See " Die Familie Mendelssohn," vol. ii.

he removed, in November, to Berlin, taking up his abode
in the family house in the Leipziger Strasse, now wholly
his own, and leaving the Gewandhaus concerts under
the temporary direction of Ferdinand Hiller. The performances at the beginning of the year had been exceptionally brilliant; including, among other attractions,
the first presentation of the *Walpurgis-Nacht*, in the
form in which we now know it—a very different form
indeed from that in which it was first presented in 1833.
Mendelssohn himself had always taken intense pleasure in
this remarkable work, and was never weary of reconsider-
ing its details, with the view of making it express, as
lucidly as possible, the intention explained to him by
Goethe. In one respect, indeed, he has commented
upon that intention in terms which it is impossible to
misunderstand. In the hymn of the Druids, which
forms the climax of the poem, Goethe clearly intends
to set forth the final revelation of everlasting truth.
Mendelssohn expresses rather the expectation of better
things, than the joy of complete religious rest. With
all its solemnity, it is but a pagan strain after all, without a trace of the perfect peace breathed in every note
of " Happy and blest are they," the Hymn of the Christian worshippers in *St. Paul.*

On the 2nd of March, a new Symphony in C minor,
by Niels W. Gade, of Copenhagen, was played with very
great success. It was the first work of this talented com-

poser that had ever been heard at the Gewandhaus, and
its cordial reception formed the first link in the chain of
events which ended in Gade's settlement in the town in
which he was destined ere long to become so great a
favourite. Towards the end of February, Berlioz visited
Leipzig, and proposed an exchange of *bâtons* with
Mendelssohn, who generously placed the entire resources of the orchestra at his disposal.[2] A little later
in the year, Joseph Joachim, then twelve years old,
visited Leipzig for the first time, played at the Gewandhaus, and laid the foundation of a life-long friendship
with the beloved Kapellmeister. In introducing these
talented artists to the public, Mendelssohn performed
a true labour of love. One of the most amiable traits in
his character was his readiness, not only to recognise
talent wherever he met with it, but to bring it promi-
nently forward; and this kindly feeling was never
more nobly expressed than in the testimonial dated
" Berlin, December 17, 1843," which he sent to Sterndale Bennett, who was then a candidate for the professorship of music at Edinburgh. It would be impossible
for one artist to pay a higher or more graceful tribute
to the genius of another than that which the leader
of the German classical school paid, in this charming

---

[2] See letter to Heller, in Berlioz's " Voyage Musical " (Paris,
1844); and his " Mémoires " (Paris, 1870).

letter, to the greatest English composer then living.[3] Unfortunately, however, Mendelssohn's estimate of the qualifications of his brother artist was very different from that entertained by the authorities of the Scottish University, who openly expressed their want of confidence in his judgment by electing another candidate.

[3] For an exact reproduction of this most interesting letter, in the original English, see the "Dictionary of Music and Musicians," vol. ii. p. 283.

CHAPTER XV.

DURING the winter of 1843—1844, Mendelssohn, having
temporarily left the Gewandhaus Concerts in charge of
his friend Ferdinand Hiller, was busily engaged at
Berlin in the preparation of a long series of compositions for the cathedral, where his influence was already
beginning to exercise a most salutary and encouraging
effect upon the Sunday and festival performances. His
connexion with the theatre was less satisfactory.

Among the works proposed to him by the King was
a musical illustration of the *Eumenides* of Æschylus,
for which he was requested to compose an overture, and
choruses similar to those which he had already furnished
for *Antigone*. He himself believed the task to be surrounded by insuperable difficulties ; and few who have
carefully studied the tragedy will fail to agree with
him as to the impossibility of successfully adapting it to
the modern stage.

With his habitual frankness, he made no attempt to
conceal his real opinion, even while doing his best to

meet his sovereign's wishes. But frankness of speech
was not in favour at the Prussian court, and his
honest doubts of success were tortured by intriguing
courtiers into a stubborn refusal to obey the royal
mandate. The result of this cruel misinterpretation was
most annoying, and tended in no small degree to
exacerbate the feeling with which he had already learned
to regard an engagement attended by chagrins fast
becoming insupportable.

But, though surrounded by enemies in Berlin, Men·
delssohn well knew where to turn for sympathy. In
February, 1844, he received from the Philharmonic
Society an invitation to direct the last six concerts of the
season. The engagement was a delightful one. Leaving his family quietly settled at Frankfort, he arrived
in London for the eighth time on the 10th of May,
once more became the guest of his old friend, Klingemann, and, on the 13th of the month, assumed command
of the famous orchestra. The season was a brilliant
one, and in addition to the interest it derived from his
presence, was rendered memorable by the first appearance in London of Ernst, Joachim, and Piatti. The chief
attractions of its varied programmes were the *Walpurgis-
Nacht*, the *Midsummer Night's Dream*, the Overtures to
Leonora (No. 1), *Egmont*, and *The Ruins of Athens*, Bach's
Orchestral Suite in D major, and Schubert's Overture
to *Fierabras*. At the last concert of the season (June

24th), Mendelssohn astounded the orchestra by his powerful rendering of the overture to *Egmont,* the *sforzandi* in
the last movement of which had never before been
correctly played in our English orchestras. It was at
this concert, also, that he played, for the first time in
England, Beethoven's Pianoforte Concerto in G major.
The effect produced by his interpretation of the five
bars of unaccompanied solo with which this great
work opens, will never be forgotten by those who were
fortunate enough to hear it. The delicacy of the *piano*
was perfect, yet every note penetrated to the remotest
corner of the room.

At the rehearsal, on Saturday the 22nd, he enriched
the first movement with a magnificent extempore *cadenza,*
in which he worked up the varied subjects of the
piece with the skill which never failed him when he
gave the reins to his exuberant fancy. On reaching
the shake at its close he found the orchestra a little
uncertain in taking up its point. In order to remove
all fear of misunderstanding, he again extemporised a
cadenza entirely different from the first, though not a
whit less beautiful. The orchestra again missed its
point so decidedly that he found it necessary to make a
third trial. This last *cadenza* was by far the longest
and most interesting of the three, and totally different,
both in matter and in style, from its predecessors. It
had, moreover, the effect of rendering the orchestral

point so safe that no fear whatever was anticipated with regard to the Monday performance.

It will be readily understood that all present looked forward to this performance with intensest excitement; feeling certain that another new *cadenza* would be improvised at the concert. And it really was so. The same subjects were placed in so different a light, that their treatment bore not the slightest shade of resemblance to the Saturday performance, until the approach of the final shake, which was so arranged as to enable the orchestra to take up its point with the most perfect accuracy.[1]

Mendelssohn played at many more concerts during the course of the London season. On the 13th of July, he rejoined his wife and children at Frankfort, and took a long holiday, which he greatly needed. On the 30th of September, he was again in Berlin, more worried than ever with the meanness of intriguing courtiers, and the blundering fatuity of jealous and incompetent officials. That the King was sincere in his desire to advance the interests of art there can be no doubt. But his good-will was neutralized by the incapacity of his advisers, and the misrepresentations of time-serving

---

[1] These four Cadences are well remembered by all who were present at the rehearsal and concert; and have, we believe, been more than once described. We give the above account on the authority of our own personal recollection of the performance; and can vouch for its accuracy in every particular.

candidates for promotion; and the situation had by this time become so intolerable, that Mendelssohn once again entreated permission to retire from office, or, at least, from all duties which would compel him to reside in the capital. To this proposal the King gave his consent. Mendelssohn's annual honorarium was reduced to 1000 thalers; and he was once more left free to live where he pleased. In accordance with this arrangement he retired in December to Frankfort, where, having entrusted the command of the Leipzig orchestra to his friend Niels W. Gade, he enjoyed some months of complete rest, declining all engagements, and only composing when inspired by ideas too tempting to resist. In this delightful state of comparative idleness he spent the greater part of the winter, with infinite benefit to his health and·spirits; and in the spring of the year 1845, the writer found him, comfortably installed, with Madame Mendelssohn and the children, in a pleasant habitation in the Grosse Bockenheimer Gasse, rejoicing in his newly-acquired liberty, and doing his best to turn it to profitable account.

CHAPTER XVI.

PERSONAL REMINISCENCES.

AFTER our first interview with Mendelssohn, in 1842, we had never ceased to hope for the privilege of being, some day, brought into more intimate relations with him, in his own country; though it was not until several years had passed, that we were supposed to be old enough to take advantage of the encouragement he had then given us. But, the right time came, at last. We knew that he never forgot: and, at the season of Pentecost, in the year 1845, we visited Germany, for the first time, well assured that he would not fail to give us the good counsel he had promised. Reaching Frankfort, at the beginning of the bright spring weather, we found him living out of doors, and welcoming the sunshine, and the flowers, with a delight as unaffected as that of the youngest of his children. On the evening of our arrival, after taking us to see Thorwaldsen's lately-finished statue of Goethe, and the poet's birthplace in the Hirschgraben, he playfully proposed that we should go to an " open-air concert," and led the way to a lonely little corner of the

H 2

public gardens, where a nightingale was singing with all its heart.

"He sings here every evening," said Mendelssohn, " and I often come to hear him. I sit here, sometimes, when I want to compose. Not that I am writing much, now; but, sometimes, I have a feeling like this "—and he twisted his hands rapidly, and nervously, in front of his breast—" and when that comes, I know that I must write. I have just finished some Sonatas for the Organ; and, if you will meet me at the Catherinenkirche, at ten o'clock to-morrow, I will play them to you."

He played them, exquisitely—the whole six, straight through, from the neatly-written MS. We remember noticing the wonderfully delicate staccato of the pedal quavers in the second movement of the Fifth Sonata, which he played upon a single 8-ft. stop, with all the crispness of Dragonetti's most highly-finished *pizzicato*.

There was only one other auditor, besides ourselves. He parted from us, at the Church door; and then Mendelssohn took us home with him, to his early dinner, with Madame Mendelssohn and the children—Karl, then seven years old, Marie, and Paul. He was full of fun, with a joke for each of the little ones; and made us all cover up the lower part of our faces, to see what animals we were like. "*Ich bin ein Adler*,"[1] he said, placing his hand in a position which made the likeness absurdly striking. Madame Mendelssohn was pro-

---

[1] " I am an eagle."

nounced to be a hare; Karl, a roebuck; Paul, a bull-finch; and we ourselves a setter. Having some business to attend to, after dinner, he left us for half an hour in his study; giving us the choice of amusing ourselves with looking through Félicien David's *Le Désert*, which had just been sent to him from Paris; or his own Pianoforte Trio in C minor, as yet unpublished, and untried. We chose the Trio; but had not found time to trace out half its beauties, before he returned, to advise with us concerning our future proceedings. "There is only one thing for you to do," he said. "Ferdinand David will be here, to-morrow, on his way back to Leipzig, from the Lower Rhine Festival, where he has been playing. I will ask him to let you travel with him. He will introduce you to all the people you will care to know. Enter yourself immediately at the Conservatorium; and get into training as soon as you possibly can. My own plans are so undecided, that I should be able to do nothing for you, here; but I am almost certain to return to Leipzig, before the end of the year, and I shall then hope to see a great deal of you."

David arrived, late that night; and, on the next evening, Mendelssohn gave a delightful little party, at which the two friends, assisted by an excellent violoncellist, played the C minor Trio, for the first time, with scarcely less effect than they afterwards produced when introducing it to the general public at the Gewandhaus. It was our last pleasant meeting in the Bockenheimer Gasse. David had arranged to start, on the next evening, for Leipzig. We met him, at the office of the Schnell-Post; and, a few moments later, Mendelssohn joined us, to say, as he was careful to express it in mixed German and English, "Not *Leben Sie wohl,* but *Auf Wiedersehn.*" He had thought of everything that could help to make the dreary diligence journey comfortable. A little basket of early fruit, for refreshment during the night ; a packet of choice cigars for David; and, for ourselves, a quite paternal scolding for insufficient defences against cold night-air. There were many last words to be said ; but so much confusion had been caused by the hurried arrival of a party of outside passengers, that, at the moment of starting, our kind friend, who had wisely retired from the scuffle, was missing. The conductor declared that he could wait no longer, and we were just giving up Mendelssohn for lost, when he suddenly reappeared, rushing round the corner of the street, with a thick woollen scarf in his hand. " Let me wrap this round your throat," he gasped, quite out of breath with his run ; "it will keep you warm in the night; and, when you get to Leipzig, you can leave it in the coach."

We need scarcely say that we did *not* "leave it in the coach." It has not been worn for many a long year ; but it lies before us, on the table, as we write its history— the dear remembrance of a very happy time.

CHAPTER XVII.

CONCERNING THE MANAGEMENT OF THE CONSERVATORIUM.

MENDELSSOHN'S prophetic spirit was not mistaken. Though he did not receive official notice of the King of Saxony's wish that he should return to Leipzig, until some weeks after our visit to Frankfurt, he no doubt knew that an intimation to that effect was on its way to him, and therefore felt no hesitation in speaking hopefully. He reappeared in the town he loved so well at the beginning of September, having previously secured a permanent residence on the first floor of a large house in the Königsstrasse, N⁰. 3 ;[1] and, on the 5th of October, he once more raised his *bâton*, at the Gewandhaus, where he was enthusiastically welcomed, with a flourish of drums and trumpets in the orchestra, and a storm of applause from the body of the hall. The first piece he conducted was the overture to *Der Freischütz*. We subjoin the entire programme, of which we have fortunately preserved a copy, as a fair example of the form of enter-

[1] Now, N⁰. 21.

tainment provided, eight-and-thirty years ago, for one of
the most appreciative audiences in Europe. It was not
the custom, at that period, to mention the conductor's
name, on the Gewandhaus programme; hence, in the
present case, that of Mendelssohn, appears only in connexion with two *Lieder ohne Worte,* though he really
directed the entire performance.

PART I.

Overture . . .	.*Der Freischütz* . .	C. M. VON WEBER.
Recit. and Aria . . .	.*Perchè non ho*	. DONIZETTI.

FRAU SCHRICKL-STEINMÜLLER.

Pianoforte Concerto, MS. . . . . . . ADOLPH HENSELT.

FRAU DR. CLARA SCHUMANN.

Scena & Aria (*Don Juan*), *Ueber Alles bleibst du theuer;* MOZART.

FRAU SCHRICKL-STEINMÜLLER.

Two *Lieder ohne Worte;* [2] MENDELSSOHN : and Fugue ; ROBERT
SCHUMANN.

FRAU DR. CLARA SCHUMANN.

PART II.

Symphony in B♭, No. 4 . . . . BEETHOVEN.

But it was not for the sake of the Gewandhaus only, that
Mendelssohn was so anxious to return to Leipzig. On the
3rd of January, 1846, he entered upon a course of active service at the Conservatorium; assuming the sole command of
two pianoforte classes, and one for composition, and in the
management of both fulfilling the duties of a hard-work-
ing professor with no less enthusiasm than that which
he had so long displayed in his character of conductor at

[2] Nos. 6 and 4, Op. 67; then fresh from the engraver's hands,
and quite unknown.

the older institution. Now that the Royal College of Music is attracting so much, and such well-merited attention in our own country, our readers may perhaps be glad to know something of the method of teaching pursued by the founder of the most important music school in Germany, on the authority of one who was fortunate enough to participate in its advantages. We shall therefore devote the remainder of our present chapter to a brief sketch of his mode of proceeding in the class-room, based on our own personal recollections, and corroborated by the contents of a MS. note-book in which we were careful to record the subjects of the various lessons, and the manner of their discussion.

Among the members of the upper classes for the study of the pianoforte and composition were, Mr. Otto Goldschmidt, Mons. Michel de Sentis, Herren Tausch, Kalliwoda, Kahlan, and Wettich, and one or two other pupils, who all met regularly, for instruction, on Wednesday and Saturday afternoons, each lesson lasting two hours. The first pianoforte piece selected for study was Hummel's Septett in D minor : and we well remember the look of blank dismay depicted upon more than one excitable countenance, as each pupil in his turn after playing the first chord, and receiving an instantaneous reproof for its want of sonority, was invited to resign his seat in favour of an equally unfortunate successor. Mendelssohn's own manner of playing grand chords, both in *forte* and *piano* passages, was peculiarly impressive ;[3] and now, when al present had tried, and failed, he himself sat down to the instrument, and explained the causes of his dissatisfaction with such microscopic minuteness, and clearness of expression, that the lesson was simply priceless. He never gave a learner the chance of mistaking his meaning ; and though the vehemence with which he sometimes expressed it made timid pupils desperately afraid of him, he was so perfectly just, so sternly impartial in awarding praise, on the one hand, and blame on the other, that consternation soon gave place to confidence, and confidence to boundless affection. Carelessness infuriated him. Irreverence for the composer he could never forgive. *" Es steht nicht da !"* [4] he almost shrieked one day to a pupil who had added a note to a certain chord. To another, who had scrambled through a difficult passage, he cried, with withering contempt, *" So spielen die Katzen!"* [5] But, where he saw an earnest desire to do justice to the work in hand, he would give direction after direction, with a lucidity which we have never heard equalled. He never left a piece until he was satisfied that the majority of the class understood it thoroughly. Hummel's Septett formed the chief part of each lesson, until the 25th of February. After that it was relieved, occasionally, by

[3] We have already alluded to this, in connexion with his powerful rendering of Beethoven's Concerto in G major, and his own, in G minor.

[4] " It is not there ! "   [5] " So play the cats ! "

one of Chopin's studies, or a Fugue from the *Wohltem-perirte Klavier*. But it was not until the 21st of March that it was finally set aside, to make room for Weber's *Concert-Stück*, the master's reading of which was superb. He would make each pupil play a portion of this great work in his own way, comment upon its delivery with the most perfect frankness, and, if he thought the player deserved encouragement, would himself supply the orchestral passages on a second pianoforte. But he never played through the piece which formed the subject of the lesson in a connected form. On a few rare occasions—we can only remember two or three—he invited the whole class to his house; and, on one of these happy days, he played an entire Sonata—but not that which the members of the class were studying. And the reason of this reticence was obvious. He wished his pupils to understand the principles by which he himself was guided in his interpretation of the works of the great masters, and at the same time to discourage servile imitation of his own rendering of any individual composition. In fact, with regard to special forms of expression, one of his most frequently reiterated maxims was, " If you want to play with true feeling, you must listen to good singers. You will learn far more from them than from any players you are likely to meet with."

Upon questions of simple *technique* he rarely touched,

except—as in the case of our first precious lesson upon
the chord of D minor—with regard to the rendering of
certain special passages. But the members of his pianoforte classes were expected to study these matters, on
other days of the week, under Herren Plaidy, or Wenzel,
professors of high repute, who had made the training of
the fingers, and wrist, their speciality. It would be impossible to over-estimate the value of this arrangement,
which provided for the acquirement of a pure touch, and
facile execution, on the one hand, while, on the other, it left
Mendelssohn free to direct the undivided attention of his
pupils to the higher branches of Art. An analogous plan
was adopted with regard to the class for composition. The
members of this simultaneously studied the technicalities
of harmony under Herr F. Richter; those of counterpoint,
and fugue, under Herr Hauptmann, the Kantor of the
Thomas-Schule, and the most learned contrapuntist in
Europe; and those of form, and instrumentation, under
Herr Niels W. Gade.

Mendelssohn himself took all these subjects into consideration, by turns, though only in their higher aspect.
For counterpoint, he employed a large black-board, with
eight red staves drawn across it. On one of these staves
he would write a *Canto fermo*; always using the soprano
clef for the soprano part.[6] Then, offering the chalk to

---

[6] No other clef was ever used at the Conservatorium for the
soprano part; nor were the students ever permitted to write alto

one of his pupils, he would bid him write a counterpoint, above, or below, the given subject. This done, he would invite the whole class to criticise the tyro's work; discussing its merits with the closest possible attention to every detail. Having corrected this, to his satisfaction, or, at least, made the best of it, he would pass on the chalk to some one else—generally, to the student who had been most severe in his criticism—bidding him add a third part to the two already written. And this process he would carry on, until the whole of the eight staves were filled. The difficulty of adding a sixth, seventh, or eighth part, to an exercise already complete in three, four, or five, and not always written with the freedom of an experienced contrapuntist, will be best understood by those who have most frequently attempted the process. It was often quite impossible to supply an additional part, or even an additional note; but Mendelssohn would never sanction the employment of a rest, as a means of escape from the gravest difficulty, until every available resource had been tried, in vain.

One day, when it fell to our own lot to write the eighth part, a certain bar presented so hopeless a deadlock, that we confessed ourselves utterly vanquished. "Cannot you find a note?" asked Mendelssohn. "Not one that could be made to fit in, without breaking a rule,"

or tenor parts in any other than their true clefs. This wholesome law was absolute in all the classes.

said we. "I am very glad," said he, in English, and laughing heartily, "for I could not find one myself." It was, in fact, a case of inevitable check-mate.

We never knew, beforehand, what form the lessons in this class would assume. Sometimes he would give out the words of a song, to be set to music, by each member of the class, before its next meeting; or a few verses of a psalm, to be set in the form of a Motet. When summoned, towards the end of May, 1846, to direct the Lower Rhine Festival, at Aix-la-Chapelle, the task he left for completion during his absence was a Quartett for stringed instruments. When any trial compositions of this kind pleased him, he had them played by the orchestral class; and would even play the viola himself, or ask Herr Gade to play it, in the chamber music;[7] striving, by every means of encouragement within his power, to promote a wholesome spirit of emulation among his pupils. It was not often that this kindly spirit met with an unworthy response; but the least appearance of ingratitude wounded him, cruelly. When the Quartetts we have mentioned were sent to him for examination, he found one of them headed "Charivari." At the next meeting of the class, he asked for an explanation of the title. "The time was

---

[7] In July, 1846, the writer enjoyed the privilege of having a Double Quartett tried in this way, the two first-violin parts being played by David and Joachim.

so short," stammered the composer, "that I found it impossible to write anything worthy of a better name. I called it 'Charivari,' to show that I knew it was rubbish." We could see that Mendelssohn felt deeply hurt; but he kept his temper nobly. "I am a very busy man,"[8] he said, "and am, just now, overwhelmed with work. Do you think you were justified in expecting me to waste my time upon a piece which you yourself knew to be 'rubbish'?[9] If you are not in earnest, I can have nothing to say to you." Nevertheless, he analysed the Quartett with quite as much care as the rest, while the culprit stood by, as white as a sheet; well knowing that not a member of the class would speak to him, for many a long day to come. In pleasant contrast to this, we cannot refrain from giving publicity to a very different story. One of the best pianoforte players in the class was a handsome young Pole, with a profusion of jet-black hair, which, in true Polish fashion, he allowed to hang half-way down his back. While playing the brilliant passages which form the climax of the *Concert-Stück*, the good fellow shook his head, one day, in such sort as to throw his rich locks over his shoulder, in a tempest of "*Kohlpechrabenschwarze Haare.*" "You must have your hair cut," said Mendelssohn, in German, with a merry laugh. The Pole was very proud of his *chevelure;* but, at the next meeting, his hair was the shortest in the class—

[8] "Ich bin ein sehr beschäftigter Mann." [9] "Dummes Zeug."

and there was not a student then present who would not gladly have had his head shaved, could he thereby have purchased the smile with which the happy student was rewarded for his devotion.

More than once, the lesson was devoted to extemporisation upon given subjects; during the course of which Mendelssohn would sit beside the *improvisatore*, and, without interrupting the performance, suggest, from time to time, certain modes of treatment which occurred to him at the moment.[1]   On other occasions, he would take two well-defined motives, and work them up into a model of the Sonata-form, in order to show how much might be accomplished by very simple means. He insisted strongly upon the importance of a natural and carefully arranged system of modulation; and would frequently call up one pupil after another to pass from a given key to some exceedingly remote one, with the least possible amount of apparent effort. On one occasion, when the writer had failed to satisfy him, in an attempt of this kind, he said, in English, " I call that modulation very ungentlemanlike."

When the lesson went well, it was easy to see that he thoroughly enjoyed it. But the work was too hard for

[1] He once gave the writer a theme, consisting simply of three Cs— a dotted quaver, a semiquaver, and a crotchet : and afterwards extemporised upon it himself ; using the three C's as the initial notes of an enchanting little melody, which he worked up into a species of *Lied ohne Worte.*

him, in addition to his other laborious duties; and the
acceptance, by Moscheles, of a pianoforte professorship at
the Conservatorium, gave him unmixed satisfaction.
But for this, the institution must have suffered terribly,
when Mendelssohn's health broke down so suddenly, after
the completion of *Elijah*.   But, when the new professor
entered upon his duties, in October, 1846, after sacrificing
his splendid position in London for the sole purpose of
doing the best he could for the interests of Art, all
anxiety on this point was at an end; and the history of
the Conservatorium, during the next twenty years, sufficiently proves the wisdom of the offer Moscheles so
generously accepted.

CHAPTER XVIII.

THE LAST SEASON AT THE GEWANDHAUS.

THE Gewandhaus season, during the winter of 1845-6, was an exceptionally brilliant one. The programmes, drawn up by Mendelssohn himself, included seven of Beethoven's Symphonies and four of Mozart's; his own new Violin Concerto, and music to *A Midsummer Night's Dream;* Schumann's Symphony in B flat; Gade's Cantata, *Comala,* produced for the first time, and many new and interesting works by other composers. Miss Dolby was engaged for ten of the subscription concerts, and achieved a great success, not only in the higher forms of classical music, but also in familiar phases of English Art then quite unknown in Germany. Indeed one of the most interesting features of the selections presented to the public was their comprehensive character. No music of any school or period was excluded, provided only that it was good, in its own peculiar style : and thus it happened, that many works were heard at the Gewandhaus, which were never, by any chance, performed elsewhere.

By command of the King of Prussia, Mendelssohn was summoned to Potsdam, on the 1st of November, 1845, for the first performance of his *Œdipus Coloneus*, and to Charlottenburg, shortly afterwards, for the production of *Athalie*. This arrangement necessarily involved his absence from some important performances at the Gewandhaus; but, on the 3rd of December, he returned to his favourite occupation, accompanied— to the delight of the public—by Mademoiselle Jenny Lind, who, though then at the height of her reputation in Berlin, had not yet been heard in Leipzig, and whose visit at that particular moment was wholly unexpected.

Mademoiselle Lind made her first appearance in the Gewandhaus at the eighth concert, on the 4th of December, 1845. Her songs—all sung, on this occasion, in German—were *Casta Diva*, and *Non mi dir*, in both of which she created a *furore;* and Mendelssohn's *Auf Flügeln des Gesanges*, and *Leise zieht durch mein Gemüth*, accompanied on the pianoforte by the composer. The last of these delightful *lieder* was twice redemanded —a circumstance quite unprecedented at the subscription concerts; and never before or since that memorable night have we heard it so superbly sung, or so deliciously accompanied.

On the following evening, 5th of December, Mendelssohn, in conjunction with his illustrious guest, gave a

concert for a charitable fund connected with the Gewandhaus orchestra; and the famous songstress deepened the
impression she had already produced, by her magnificent
interpretation of *Wie nahte mir der Schlummer*, the solo
passages in the great Finale to *Euryanthe*, an Aria
from *Figaro*, and some Swedish Melodies with pianoforte accompaniment. Mendelssohn's own contributions
to this performance were his First Concerto in G minor,
and a *Solo für Pianoforte*, which consisted of two *Lieder
ohne Worte*—No 1. Book VI. and No 6. Book V.—both
evidently chosen on the spur of the moment, and rendered
intensely interesting by a prelude and interlude such
as he alone could have improvised. During the course
of a long and masterly modulation from the key of
E flat to that of A major he carried on the quiet semiquaver accompaniment of the first *lied* for some considerable time, without interruption, treating it with new
and unexpected harmonies so contrived as to permit the
continuance of the bell-like B flat in the form of an inverted pedal-point, and always presenting the reiterated
note in some novel and captivating position. As the
modulation proceeded, the B flat gave place to other
notes, treated in like manner; and presently these were
relieved by a new figure, which rapidly developed into
the well-known feathery arpeggio of the famous *Früh-
lingslied*. Every one thus knew what was coming: but
no one was prepared for the fiery treatment which first

worked up this arpeggio-form into a stormy climax
carrying all before it, and then as it gradually approached
the long-expected chord of A major, died gently away,
in a long-drawn *diminuendo,* so artfully managed,
that, when the delicious melody was at last fairly introduced, it sent an electric thrill through every heart
in the room. This was indeed a "gentlemanlike modulation," never to be forgotten by any one who heard it.

On her return home after the concert, Mademoiselle
Lind was greeted by 300 enthusiastic amateurs, with a
serenade, sung beneath her windows by torchlight. A
large band of wind instruments took part in the performance; and after its conclusion, Mendelssohn, who
stood beside Mademoiselle Lind on a balcony, gracefully
thanked the serenaders, in her name, for the pleasure
they had given her. On the following day she returned
to Berlin, but again visited Leipzig in the early spring,
and on the 12th of April (Easter Sunday), gave a
chamber concert at the Gewandhaus, in which, accompanied by Mendelssohn, she sang Pacini's *Il soave e ben
contento,* Mozart's *Non mi dir,* Weber's *Glöcklein im
Thale,* and *Und ob die Wolke,* and a second selection of
Swedish Airs.

This concert is sadly memorable as the last at which
Mendelssohn played publicly in Leipzig. The pieces he
had selected were Beethoven's Violin Sonata in G major,
in which he was assisted by David; the same composer's

Sonata in C sharp minor; and, last of all, one of his own *Lieder ohne Worte*, which, however, was played by Madame Schumann. Although this lady's name did not appear in the programme, Mendelssohn, seeing her among the audience, invited her to take his place; a compliment which she gracefully acknowledged by playing the *Lied ohne Worte*, No. 4, Book VI., and a *Scherzo* of her own.[1]

On the last day of the old year, 1845, Mendelssohn gave at his residence in the Königsstrasse, one of those delightful musical evenings, the memory of which is so dear to all who were privileged to share his hospitality. He began by playing Beethoven's Sonata in E major, Op. 109, with the lovely aria and variations to which he alone of all the *virtuosi* we have heard, knew how to do full justice. Miss Dolby sang, *Sun of the sleepless, There be none of beauty's daughters,* and Handel's, *If guiltless blood be your intent.* David played Mendelssohn's Violin Concerto to the composer's pianoforte accompaniment. And Madame Schumann played some caprices, and a canon by her husband, who was present, but in accordance with his usual custom took no active part in the proceedings. A perfect little

---

[1] The last notes actually played by Mendelssohn in the Gewandhaus were those of the accompaniment to Mademoiselle Lind's Swedish Airs. Our recollection of the circumstances is corroborated by an entry in a note-book which we kept at this period.

supper was then served, at a number of small tables, placed in different parts of the room, and as the clock struck twelve, the beloved host rose, glass in hand, from his seat, and, passing from table to table, touched the glass of every guest in turn, pledging each one with his indescribable smile, in some choice old *Rhein-wein* which had been specially reserved for the occasion.[2]

It was a happy moment. We little thought that the New Year's Day of 1846 was the last but one our host was destined to spend on earth !

[2] Though drinking very little wine himself, Mendelssohn thoroughly understood the merits of a precious vintage, and delighted in setting its produce before his guests. He was an accomplished concocter of *Maitrank*, a kind of " cup" made with various kinds of Hock and Moselle, cunningly mixed in certain artistic proportions, flavoured with fresh sprigs of *Waldmeister* (Woodroof), and sweetened with sugar. He once fabricated, at the house of his brother-in-law, Herr Schunck, a bowl of *Maitrank* which was pronounced by all the connoisseurs present to be the finest on record ; and he was justly proud of the nectar he distributed. He himself, using a familiar German expression, pronounced it to be " *Der wahre Jakob* "—a phrase which, for the writer's instruction, he laughingly translated into English, as, " The true Jack."

CHAPTER XIX.

" ELIJAH."

UNHINDERED by the labours of this busy winter, *Elijah* was steadily approaching completion. The first part was finished on the 23rd of May, 1846 ; before the end of July, the whole was sent to England, for translation from the German—in which language the book was originally compiled—by Messrs. Bartholomew and Klingemann. Yet, time was also found for the fulfilment of other very important engagements. The *Lauda Sion,* written for the festival of *Corpus Christi,* at Liege, was finished on the 10th of February, though the performance did not take place until the 11th of June, when Mendelssohn conducted it in person, after having presided at the Lower Rhine Festival, at Aix-la-Chapelle (on the 31st of May and the 2nd of June), and a concert at Dusseldorf. On the 5th of August, he organised a preliminary rehearsal of the new Oratorio in Leipzig. Soon after this he started on his journey to England. And on the 18th he arrived, for the ninth time, in London, and once more became the guest of Klingemann, at the well-known house in Hobart Place.

The first rehearsal of *Elijah*, in England, was a private trial, with pianoforte accompaniment, at Moscheles' house. Two full rehearsals then took place at the Hanover Square Rooms; and nothing that could conduce to the excellence of the final performance was left undone, though the amount of work compressed into the time at command was excessive. Mendelssohn looked very worn and nervous, yet he would suffer no one to relieve him, even in the scrutiny of the orchestral parts, which he himself spread out on some benches beneath the windows on the left-hand side of the room, and insisted upon sorting out and examining for himself.[1] On the 23rd he went down to Birmingham, where he conducted two full rehearsals, on the 24th and 25th and on Wednesday, the 26th of August, the oratorio was for the first time performed in public.

It would be impossible to describe the enthusiasm with which *Elijah* was received at Birmingham. The performance was admirable. Mendelssohn himself spoke

---

[1] He was always particularly anxious on this point. The principal copyist in London in those days was a well-known man, whose name was constantly called out at rehearsals when parts were missing. One day, when some parts were missing at a Gewandhaus rehearsal, Mendelssohn turned round, laughing heartily, and called out this man's name, to the astonishment of the Germans, who could not see the point of the joke.

of it in terms of the highest approval, and was especially delighted with Herr Staudigl—whose rendering of the part of Elijah has never yet been equalled—and Mr. Lockey. The principal soprano and contralto parts were sung by Miss Birch and Miss M. B. Hawes; and the choruses were sung with wonderful precision for a first performance. Eleven pieces were redemanded. Artists and audience vied with each other in their endeavour to increase the roar of applause which, at the close of the first and second parts, was simply deafening : and, when all was over, those who had taken part in the proceedings rushed madly forward in the hope of exchanging a word with the hero of the day, who heartily grasped every hand that came within his reach, and thanked all present for their share in the performance with which he was so deeply gratified.

When the festival was over, Mendelssohn returned to London, with Mr. and Mrs. Moscheles; spent a few days at Ramsgate with his friend Mr. Benecke; and, on the 6th of September, crossed, with Staudigl, to Ostend, whence he proceeded by easy stages to Leipzig; not, as might be supposed, to rest, but, with the least possible delay, to remodel the Oratorio, with which he was very far from satisfied, notwithstanding the pleasure he had derived from its first performance. Scarcely a movement of *Elijah* passed unchanged through the fire of this sweeping revision, the extent of which can only be thoroughly understood by a comparison of the original MS. score with the published copy; but it was not until the whole was completed that the music was given out to the engravers, and not until the month of July, 1847, that the complete edition was issued to the public by Messrs. Simrock.

By command of the King of Prussia, a considerable portion of Mendelssohn's time was devoted, during the autumn of 1846, to the service of the Cathedral at Berlin. In October, Moscheles came to Leipzig, and relieved him from much anxiety with regard to the direction and conduct of the Conservatorium. The arrival of this trusty and affectionate friend was most opportune, for troubles were multiplying rapidly. Not the least among them was a highly unsatisfactory correspondence with Mr. Lumley, the lessee of Her Majesty's Theatre, concerning the preparation of an Opera, for which Scribe was engaged to furnish a libretto, founded on Shakespeare's *Tempest*. The scheme fell through hopelessly, as might have been expected, for it is impossible to believe that any kind of sympathy could ever have existed between the composer and the dramatist. Moreover Geibel, the German poet, was simultaneously engaged upon the fabrication of another libretto, founded upon the Legend of *Loreley*, with which Mendelssohn seems to have been better satisfied; and, in addition to this, he was already contemplating a new Oratorio, to be called

Christus. The demands upon his time and thought
were, therefore, excessive; and it is not to be wondered
at that he once more committed the direction of the
Gewandhaus concerts to his friend Gade; only conducting one occasionally towards the close of the season,
and never consenting to play in public. Yet, in January,
1847, he instituted a most minute examination of the
students at the Conservatorium, sparing neither time
nor labour in his endeavour to make it as complete as
possible: and, on the 2nd of April, he conducted a performance of *St. Paul.*

All these events were, however, of small importance,
compared with an engagement into which he had entered
with the Sacred Harmonic Society, for the reproduction
of *Elijah,* in its revised form, at Exeter Hall. In fulfilment of this, he crossed the Channel with Joachim, on
the 12th of April; and, on the evening of that day,
arrived, for the tenth time, in London, the welcome
guest of his friend Klingemann, whose house in Hobart
Place had so often received him during his visits to this
country.

The extensive changes which had been made in the
Oratorio since its first performance added greatly to the
labour attendant upon its reproduction, but it was not
in his nature to leave his work half-done. The performances originally arranged for the 16th, 23rd, and 28th
of April were so brilliantly successful, that a fourth was

organised for the 30th. On the 23rd the Queen and
Prince Consort were present; and the Prince wrote on
his programme a memorandum, in which he compared
Mendelssohn's zealous defence of the true principles of
Art, and condemnation of its false corrupters, to Elijah's
condemnation of the worshippers of Baal.

In addition to these four performances of the oratorio,
Mendelssohn conducted it at Manchester, on the 20th
of April; and at Birmingham on the 27th. On the 26th
he conducted the *Scotch Symphony*, and the music of
A Midsummer Night's Dream, at the Philharmonic concert,
in the presence of the Queen; and also played, for the
second time, Beethoven's Pianoforte Concerto in G major,
introducing an extempore *cadenza* no less interesting
than that of the year 1844, though, in consequence of a
less perfect understanding with the conductor, he found
it necessary to hold up his hand in order to prevent the
orchestra from bringing in the *a tempo* before he had
completely worked out his idea.

There can be no doubt that Mendelssohn's health
was by this time seriously, if not hopelessly, impaired.
Though no one suspected the terrible gravity of the
case, or the fatal extent to which his physical powers
had been undermined by excessive mental labour, it was
evident that he was working himself to death. We
ourselves have always dated the change from the first
production of *Elijah*, in 1846; and believed it to have

been the result, not of the labour of composing, but of that of producing this, his last great work. When talking with him, on the day before the first full rehearsal, in Mr. Klingemann's study, we were startled for the first time by a worn look, quite foreign to his usual expression—a look of pain, which was even more distressingly apparent on the following morning, as he stood beneath the side windows of the Hanover Square Rooms, arranging the orchestral parts of the Oratorio in the order proper for their distribution.[2] Eight months had passed since then, and now the change was patent to every one. Yet his dauntless spirit supported him wonderfully through the labours of this busy time. Six performances of *Elijah*, one of the *Scotch Symphony* and *Midsummer Night's Dream*, and a magnificent rendering of Beethoven's Concerto, between the 16th and the 30th of April! On the 1st of May he played to the Queen and the Prince Consort for two hours at Buckingham Palace. On the 4th he played at a concert of the Beethoven Quartett Society, his Trio in C minor—the Frankfort Trio—and some *Lieder ohne Worte*. On that evening Mademoiselle Jenny Lind made her first appearance at Her Majesty's Theatre in *Roberto il Diavolo*, and he was there to witness his friend's first triumph in England. On the 5th he played an Organ Fugue at the "Concert

[2] See page 121.

of Antient Music." On the 6th he played to a large
party at the Prussian Embassy. On the 8th he took leave
of the Queen and Prince Consort; and in the evening
started with the Klingemanns on his homeward journey.

At Herbesthal, the well-known station on the Prussian frontier, he was subjected to inexpressible annoy-
ance by an officious member of the police force, who
mistook him for a political offender endeavouring to
escape from justice. In his then weak condition, this
miserable blunder, which, under other circumstances,
would have cost him no more than an evanescent burst of
just indignation, became a source of serious discomfort.

He arrived in Frankfurt, weary and ill, irritable to
the last degree, and in a state of physical exhaustion
which caused the gravest anxiety to his family, though
it was hoped that rest alone, if it could but be secured,
would suffice to restore the shattered nerves, and repair
the injury caused by so long a period of uninterrupted
exertion. But there was no rest at hand. In place of
it, he was summoned, without a moment's preparation,
to bear the most terrible shock he had ever yet been
called upon to sustain. What wonder that neither
mind nor body were equal to the trial! What wonder
that he was crushed by a blow which would have
affected him most severely at any time, but from which
no other than a fatal result could possibly have been
anticipated, in his then state of exhaustion and distress!

CHAPTER XX.

THE END.

On Friday afternoon, the 14th of May, 1847, Madame
Hensel, the beloved sister Fanny, to whom, from earliest
infancy, Felix, the child, the boy, the man, had committed every secret of his beautiful art-life; the kindred
spirit, with whom he had shared his every dream before his first attempt to translate it into sound; the
faithful friend, who had been more to him than any
other member of the happy circle in the Leipziger
Strasse, of which, from first to last, she was the very
life and soul—Fanny Hensel, the sister, the artist, the
poet, while conducting a rehearsal of the music for the
next bright Sunday gathering, was suddenly seized with
paralysis; suffered her hands to fall, powerless, from the
piano at which she had so often presided; and, an hour
before midnight, was called away to join the beloved
parents whose death had been as sudden, and pain-
less, as her own. She had hoped and prayed that
she too might pass away as they had done. And

her prayer was granted : to her exceeding gain ; but to the endless grief of the brother who had loved her as himself. On Sunday morning, in place of the piano, a coffin, covered with flowers, stood in the well-known hall in the Garden House. And the life, of which that Garden House had so long been the cherished home, became henceforth a memory of the past.

Mendelssohn had been but two days in Frankfort when the sad news was, all too suddenly, communicated to him. With a terrible cry he fell fainting to the ground; and never again did his merry laugh gladden the hearts of the friends to whose pleasure it had so often contributed in the happy days when it was a joy, even to see him smile. For some weeks he remained utterly prostrated by the unexpected blow; but in June he was thought well enough to remove, with his family to Baden Baden, where he was joined by his brother Paul, and his sorrowing brother-in-law. The whole party then moved slowly on towards Switzerland, passing by Schaffhausen and Lucerne, to Interlaken, where they remained for some little time. A month later, Felix was still unable even to write a letter. But, about this time, he began some water-colour drawings, in which he soon took so real an interest, that they not only served to divert his mind, but enabled him to make great advances in an art which he had always cultivated with intense pleasure. Paul and Hensel returned home in

K

July; but Felix remained at Interlaken with his family until September, gradually returning to his old habits; writing, among other music, the beautiful Quartett in F minor (Op. 80), with some portions of *Loreley*, and of the new oratorio, *Christus*; and giving the best attention he could to proposals for the future, the most important of which was a commission from the Philharmonic Society for a new Symphony. Mr. Chorley, who spent some days with him towards the end of August, has left us a touching picture of his life at this period,[1] recalling so much, and yet so little, of the happiness of well-remembered days, now passed away for ever. So much sweet warmth, and gentle *bonhomie*; so very, very little of the brightness destined ere long to vanish into night. "We have resolved to come here every year," he said, while sitting beneath the pine-trees on the Hohenbühl. Then breaking off suddenly, and putting his hand to his head, he added, "But what is the use of planning anything? I shall not live."

By the 17th of September he was again in Leipzig; and played for some time on a new grand pianoforte, sent to him by Messrs. Broadwood. This gave him great pleasure; and he would often, when interested in his work, seem to forget himself, for the moment, and speak hopefully, and even cheerfully, of the future. But a week spent at Berlin reopened the wound that

[1] "Modern German Music," vol. ii.

had already so fatally shattered his constitution, and was wearing his life away, with a merciless rapidity, which those who were nearest and dearest to him persistently refused to look fairly and honestly in the face. It is impossible to believe that these dear ones could have been really blind to the truth. Though they dared not confess it, even to themselves, it must have been impressed upon them, every moment, if only by the change in his accustomed habits. Contrary to all previous experience, he dreaded all contact with the public. When the Gewandhaus concerts began, on the 3rd of October, he left the whole management of them in the hands of his friend Julius Rietz, taking no share even in the arrangement of the programmes. The only event of the kind in which he seemed to take any interest, was a projected performance of *Elijah,* at Vienna, in which Mademoiselle Lind was to sing, and which he had promised to conduct. But this, alas! was not to be. On the 9th of October, after walking with Moscheles in the Rosenthal,[2] he called on Madame Frege, and accompanied her in his last set of Songs (Op. 71). He asked her to repeat them. She left the room, to order lights; and on her return found him shivering, and suffering from violent pain in the head. He was taken home, to bed; and the attack proved very serious: but he rallied, after some days, and,

[2] A woody spot, in the suburbs of Leipzig, and a favourite resort of its inhabitants.

on the 28th, walked out with Madame Mendelssohn, dining heartily afterwards. This improvement, however, was followed by a still more violent attack, after which he remained, for a long time, perfectly unconscious. And now, not only his friends, but the whole town, became alive to the dreadful truth; which, indeed, could no longer be concealed. For a short time, he so far recovered consciousness as to recognise those who stood by him, and to answer a few questions: but another relapse took place, on the 3rd of November, and after this he never spoke again. During the greater part of the next day the state of unconsciousness continued, without apparent suffering. Beside the bed watched Madame Mendelssohn, her brother-in-law Paul, Ferdinand David, Moscheles, and Dr. Schleinitz; but all hope of saving the beloved husband, brother, and friend had long since perished; and at 9.24 p.m. on Thursday, the 4th of November, 1847, he died.

On Friday and Saturday "hundreds of mourners pressed into the house, for one last look at the familiar features; and the family, with noble generosity, placed no barrier in the way."[3] On Sunday, at 4. p.m., the coffin was borne to the Paulinenkirche, preceded by a band of wind instruments, playing the *Lied ohne Worte* in E minor, Book V. No. 3, scored, for the occasion, by Moscheles. Immediately after the band

---

[3] Lampadius, ch. xiv.

followed the then senior student of the Conservatorium, Mons. de Sentis, bearing a cushion, on which were placed Mendelssohn's *Ordre pour le mérite*, and a silver crown, the offering of his pupils. The pall, almost hidden beneath a mass of palm-branches and flowers, was borne by Schumann, David, Gade, Hauptmann, Moscheles, and Rietz. Before the bier walked the members of the Gewandhaus Orchestra, the choir of the Thomas-Schule, the choral societies of the city, and the professors and students of the Conservatorium : behind it followed the chief-mourner, Paul Mendelssohn-Bartholdy, and the rest of the family, the clergy of the city, the university professors, a large body of military and civil officers, and a long procession of friends and uninvited mourners, all anxious to pay their last act of reverence to the great tone-poet whom they had not—as is too often the case— forgotten to honour, while he yet lived to acknowledge and to value their proferred homage. On its arrival in the church, the coffin was placed on a *catafalque* surrounded by six tall wax tapers. Mons. de Sentis laid the crown at the master's feet, while the whole congregation joined in *Errett mich, o mein lieber*. During the course of the service, the choir sang the Choral, *To Thee, O Lord, I yield my spirit*, and the chorus, *Happy and blest are they*, from *St. Paul*. A sermon was preached by Pastor Howard, the minister of the Reformed Congregation, and the ceremony concluded with the last chorus from Sebastian Bach's *Passion according to St. Matthew*.

When the whole congregation had left the Church, a lady entered, in deep mourning, and kneeled beside the coffin. It was Cecile, Madame Mendelssohn, who, amidst the awful stillness of the deserted building, took her last farewell of the husband she had loved so well.

At 10 p.m., the coffin was taken to the railway station, and conveyed to Berlin. At Cöthen, the local choir awaited it, in the night, with music; and, at Dessau, the aged Friedrich Schneider brought his own well-trained choir, at half-past one o'clock a.m., to sing a Hymn which he had written for the occasion. At 7 a.m., on Monday, the 8th of November, it arrived at Berlin, where the Cathedral Choir received it with the Chorale, *Jesu, meine Freude*. The sun was rising, as it was borne into the Alte Dreifaltigkeits-Kirchhof, just without the Halle Gate, where it was deposited in its last resting-place, in front of the tombs of Abraham and Leah Mendelssohn-Bartholdy, and beside that of Madame Hensel, in the family vault, after a second service, during the course of which Pastor Berduschek delivered a funeral oration, and the members of the Singakademie sang a Hymn composed for the occasion by Grell. The grave is now marked by a Cross, bearing the inscription :—

"*Jakob Ludwig Felix Mendelssohn-Bartholdy ; geboren*

zu Hamburg, am 3 *Feb.*, 1809 *; gestorben zu Leipzig, am* 4 *Nov.*, 1847."

It was but a very little time afterwards that the vault was again opened for Mendelssohn's youngest boy, Felix, who now lies by his side. Madame Mendelssohn survived her husband nearly six years, dying of consumption, on Sunday, the 25th of September, 1853, at Frankfort, where she lies in the beautiful God's-acre overlooking the Taunus Gebirge.

CHAPTER XXI.

MENDELSSOHN'S POSITION IN ART.

IN order fully to understand the genius of Mendelssohn
and fairly to estimate its influence upon the contempo-
rary and subsequent progress of Art in Germany and
other countries, we must carefully consider the condition
of Music at the moment of his entrance into public
life.

Weber produced his last great work—*Oberon*—and
died, during its first successful run, when Mendelssohn
was seventeen years old. For some years after this
event, German Art was worthily represented by Spohr
alone; and it is certain that, great as was the respect
with which Mendelssohn and Spohr regarded each other,
neither of them, from first to last, ever exercised the
slightest appreciable influence upon the other's artistic
career. They were great friends. We well remember
how, when Spohr visited Leipzig, in 1846, he was everywhere received with the honour due to an artist of the
highest rank. At the Conservatorium, all the elder pupils

were paraded before him in turn; and his own *Weihe der Töne* was played to him, in the Orchestral Class, by the Stringed Band of the institution, the wind parts being filled in, as usual, on two pianofortes, at one of which the writer had the honour to sit. At a private party given by Madame Voigt, his own Double Quartett in E Minor was played, as it had probably never been played before; he himself leading the first division, and David the second, while Mendelssohn and Gade played the two Viole, and Joachim the Second Violin of the first section.[1] And the enthusiasm with which the illustrious guest was everywhere received was entirely the result of Mendelssohn's undisguised admiration for his genius. Yet it is not too much to say that between that genius and his own there existed no affinity whatever.

In France, the ruling power in Mendelssohn's early days was Auber, whose Operas he held in the utmost possible aversion.[2] In Italy, Rossini still reigned supreme, even after he had long ceased to write for the Italian Stage. Of young composers, coming to the front with reasonable prospect of carrying on the work of the departed giants, there were none.

---

[1] The only other occasion on which we have heard this beautiful work played with anything like equal effect was at the "Beethoven Rooms," in 1847, when Spohr led the first division, and Joachim the second.

[2] See page 24.

What wonder, then, that Mendelssohn, feeling the Divine Fire within him, stood forth as the champion of the Art he loved, and did battle bravely against the false partisans, who, pretending to advance it, were in reality its bitterest enemies! and what wonder that the world, seeing him in earnest, and attracted by his varied and unquestionable talents, learned first to recognise, and afterwards to worship them!

The style he cultivated was, in every sense of the expression, his own; yet we should be led grievously astray were we to regard it as a new invention. It was the natural development of a well-defined system of progress. A continuation of good work, begun by his predecessors, and founded upon the principles they inculcated. His method of Part-writing was, in all essential points, identical with that evolved by Sebastian Bach from the Counterpoint of the 16th century. His forms were moulded, conscientiously, though never servilely, on the lines laid down by Haydn; the normal severity of the primitive design being everywhere tempered with the freedom introduced into it, with so great success, by Beethoven, and practised by all later writers without exception. In his rich and varied Instrumentation, he availed himself of all the resources of the modern Orchestra; and, if he did not write for the Voice, like Mozart, or Cimarosa, he at least understood its capabilities thoroughly. But in none of these technical per-

fections is his own peculiar idiosyncrasy—his inmost
self—manifested with sufficient certainty to establish
the identity of his productions beyond dispute. If we
would discover this, we must seek for it in his method
of phrasing. The perfect balance maintained between
the various members of his musical sentences is strikingly
characteristic. It would be impossible, in a sketch like
the present, to analyse this peculiarity in detail, but
those conversant with Mendelssohn's works can scarcely
have failed to notice it; and we need only direct the
attention of others, who have not made them a special
study, to the structure of the first *Allegro* of the *Scotch
Symphony*, or of the various Subjects of the *Overture to
Ruy Blas*, in order to make our meaning clear.

The experienced student of Mendelssohn's works finds,
in the construction of these Subjects, sufficient evidence
to prove their authorship beyond all possibility of
doubt; while the tyro may study them with equal
pleasure and advantage.

COMPLETE CATALOGUE OF MENDELS-SOHN'S WORKS.

(Arranged in Chronological Order.[1])

Op. 1. First Quartett for P.F. and Str. Instr., in C Min. (Ded. to Count Anton von Radziwill) [1822].

Op. 2. Second Quartett for P.F. and Str. Instr., in F Min. (Ded. to Zelter) [1823].

Op. 10.[2] *Die Hochzeit des Camacho* ("The Marriage of Camacho"), Comic Opera in two acts [1824].

Op. 11. First Symphony, in C Min. (originally numbered xiii.) (Ded. to the Philharmonic Society) [1824].

Op. 3. Third Quartett for P.F. and Str. Instr., in B Min. (Ded. to Goethe) [1825].

Op. 4. Sonata for P.F. and Vn., in F Min. (Ded. to E. Ritz).

Op. 5. *Capriccio* for P.F., in F sharp Min. [1825].

Op. 6. Sonata for P.F., in E [1826].

Op. 7. *Sieben Charakterstücke* for P.F. (Ded. to Ludwig Berger).

Op. 8. Twelve Songs [the 12th for two voices]. (Nos. 2, 3, and 12 by Fanny Hensel.)

Op. 9. Twelve Songs, "The Youth and the Maiden." (Nos. 7, 10, and 12 by Fanny Hensel.)

Op. 21.[3] Concert-Overture, No. 1., "A Midsummer Night's Dream," in E [1826].

---

[1] On the authority of Breitkopf and Härtel's "Thematic Catalogue" (Leipzig, 1873). The dates are those of composition. Where no year is given the MS. is undated.

[2] It will be seen that in this and some other important cases, we have sacrificed the order of the *Opus*-numbers to the more interesting date of production.

[3] See the preceding footnote.

Op. 12. First Quartett for Str. Instr., in E flat [1829].
Op. 13. Second Quartett for Str. Instr., in A [1827].
Op. 14. *Rondo Capriccioso* for P.F., in E [Dated "Oct. 26."].
Op. 15. *Fantasie* for P.F. (on "The Last Rose of Summer").
Op. 16. Three *Fantasies* [4] or *Caprices*:—
 No. 1. *Rosen und Nelken in Menge* (Andante and Allegro, in A) [1829].
 No. 2. *Der Kleine Fluss* ("The Rivulet"), in E [1829].
 No. 3. *Ecremocarpus*, (*Capriccio* in E Min.) [1829].
Op. 17. *Variations Concertantes* for P.F. and Cello, in D (Ded. to Paul Mendelssohn-Bartholdy) [1829].
Op. 19. *Sechs Lieder ohne Worte*, for P.F., Bk. 1 [No. 6 dated "Venice, 1830"].
Op. 19 *bis*. Six Songs [No. 6 dated 1830].
Op. 39. Three Motets for Female Voices, with Organ [1830].
Op. 18. First Quintett for Str. (2 *Viole*) [1831].
Op. 20. *Ottetto* for Str., in E flat (Ded. to E. Ritz).
Op. 22. *Capriccio Brillante* for P.F. and Orch. in B Min.
Op. 23. Church Music, with Organ Accomp.:—
 Aus tiefer Noth.
 Ave Maria, à 8.
 Mitten wir, à 8.
Op. 24. Overture for Wind Instr., in C.
Op. 25. First Concerto for P.F., in G Min. (Ded. to Fräulein D. von Schauroth).
Op. 26. Concert-Overture, No. 2, *Fingal's Höhle* [called also "The Hebrides," "Fingal's Cave," and "The Isles of Fingal"] in B Min. (Ded. to Franz Hauser).
Op. 27. Concert-Overture, No. 3, *Die Meeresstille und Glückliche Fahrt* ("The Calm Sea and Prosperous Voyage"), in D.
Op. 31. Psalm cxv., for Solo, Chorus, and Orch. [1830].
Op. 32. Concert-Overture, No. 4, *Die Schöne Melusine* ("The Lovely Melusina") [1833].
Op. 33. Three Caprices for P.F., in A Min., E, and B flat Min. (Ded. to Klingemann) [1833].
Op. 28. *Sonate Ecossaise*, Fantasia for P.F., in F sharp Min. (Ded. to Moscheles) [1833].
Op. 29. *Rondo Brillante* for P.F. and Orch., in E flat (Ded. to Moscheles) [1834].
Op. 30. *Sechs Lieder ohne Worte*, for P.F., Bk. 2 (Ded. to Fräulein Elise von Woringen) [1833—1837].
Op. 34. Six Songs, (No. 5 Ded. to Fräulein Julie Jeanrenaud—Madame Schunck) [1824].

[4] See page 41.

Op. 35. Six Preludes and Fugues for P.F. : —
    No. 1, in E Min.[5]
    No. 2, in D [Prel. 1836].
    No. 3, in B Min. [1832].
    No. 4, in A flat [1835].
    No. 5, in F Min. [Prel., 1836 ; Fu., 1834].
    No. 6, in B flat [Prel., 1837 ; Fu., 1836].
Op. 36. St. Paul, Oratorio, [1836].
Op. 37. Three Preludes and Fugues for the Organ (Ded. to
    Thomas Attwood) [1837] :—
    No. 1, in C Min.
    No. 2, in G.
    No. 3, in D Min.
Op. 38. *Sechs Lieder ohne Worte,* for P.F., Bk. 3 (Ded. to Fräu-
    lein R. von Woringen) [1836—1837].
Op. 40. Second Concerto for P.F. in D Min. [1837].
Op. 41. Open-Air Music, first set of Six Part-Songs for
    S.A.T.B. [1834].
Op. 42. Psalm xlii., for Chorus and Orchestra.
Op. 43. Serenade and *Allegro giojoso,* for P.F. and Orch., in
    B Min. [1838].
Op. 44. Third, Fourth, and Fifth Quartetts for Str. Instr.
    (Ded. to Prince of Sweden) :—
    No. 3, in D [1838].
    No. 4, in E Min. [1837].
    No. 5, in E flat [1838].
Op. 45. First Sonata for P.F. and Cello, in B flat [1838].
Op. 46. Psalm xcv., Solo, Chorus and Orch. [1838].
Op. 47. Six Songs (Ded. to Frau C. Schleinitz) [1839].
Op. 48. Open-air Music, second set of Six Part-Songs (Ded. to
    Dr. Martin and Dr. Speirs) [1839].
Op. 49. First Trio for P.F., Vn. and Cello, in D Min [1839].
Op. 50. Six Part-Songs, for Male Voices (No. 2, *Der Jäger
    Abschied,* "The Hunter's Farewell"), with Accomp. for 4
    Horns and Bass Trombone; the rest unaccompanied.
    (Ded. to the *Liedertafel* in Leipzig) [1839—1840].
Op. 51. Psalm civ., for 8 Voices and Orch. (Ded. to J. W.
    Schirmer).
Op. 52. *Lobgesang,* "*Sinfonia-Cantata, No.* 1." Called also the
    "Second Symphony." (Ded. to King Friedrich August of
    Saxony) [1840].
Op. 53. *Sechs Lieder ohne Worte,* for P.F., Bk. 4 (Ded. to Miss.
    Sophie Horsley) [1841].
Op. 54. Seventeen *Variations sérieuses,* for P.F., in D Min. [1840].
                  [5] See page 34.

Op. 55. Music to the *Antigone* of Sophocles, for Chorus of Male Voices and Orch. (Ded. to King Friedrich Wilhelm IV. of of Prussia) [1841].

Op. 56. Third Symphony, in A Min., called "The Scotch Symphony" (Ded. to Queen Victoria [6]) [1843].

Op. 57. Six Songs (Ded. to Frau Livia Frege) [1829—1841].

Op. 58. Second Sonata for P.F. and Cello (Ded. to Count Matthias Wielhorsky).

Op. 59. Open-Air Music, third Set of Six Part-Songs for S.A.T.B. (Ded. to Frau Henriette Benecke) [1837—1843].

Op. 60. *Die Erste Walpurgis-Nacht,* Ballad for Chorus and Orch. [First version, dated 1831—1832. The second version was not produced until 1843].

Op. 61. The Incidental Music to "A Midsummer Night's Dream" (Ded. to Dr. Heinrich Conrad Schleinitz).

Op. 62. *Sechs Lieder ohne Worte,* for P.F., Bk. 5 (Ded. to Frau Clara Schumann) [1842—1844].

Op. 63. Six Two-Part Songs [1836—1844].

Op. 64. Concerto for Violin and Orchestra, in E Min. [1844].

Op. 65. Six Sonatas for the Organ [7] (Ded. to Dr. F. Schlemmer) [1844—1845].

Op. 66. Second Trio for P.F., Vn. and Cello in C. Min. (Ded. to L. Spohr) [Composed at Frankfort in 1845].[8]

Op. 67. *Sechs Lieder ohne Worte,* for P.F., Bk. 6 (Ded. to Fräulein Sophie Rosen) [1843—1845].

Op. 68. *Festgesang,* Schiller's Poem, "*An die Künstler,*" for Male Voices, with Accomp. of Brass Instr.

Op. 69. Three Motets, for a Solo Voice and Chorus [1847].

Op. 70. Elijah, Oratorio.

Op. 71. Six Songs (among them the *Nachtlied,* Mendelssohn's last composition, written as a birthday-present for Dr. Schleinitz, Oct. 1st, 1847).[9]

Op. 72. Six Children's Pieces for P.F. [1845—1847].

The following compositions were published posthumously :—

Op. 73 (Op. 1, Posth.). *Lauda Sion,* Hymn for Chorus and Orch. [1846].

Op. 74 (Op. 2, Posth.). Music to Racine's *Athalie* [Overture, 1844—1845; Chor., 1843].

Op. 75 (Op. 3, Posth.). Four Part-Songs for Male Voices. Second Set [1839—1844].

Op. 76 (Op. 4, Posth.). Four Part-Songs for Male Voices. Third Set [1844—1846].

[6] See page 86. The Second Symphony is the *Lobgesang* (Op. 52), called, in the English Edition, "*Sinfonia-Cantata, No. 1.*"

[7] See page 100.   [8] See page 101.   [9] See page 131.

Op. 77 (Op. 5, Posth.). Three Vocal Duets [1836, 1839, 1847].
Op. 78 (Op. 6, Posth.). Psalms ii., xxii., and xliii., Solo and Chor. [1844].
Op. 79 (Op. 7, Posth.). Six Motets for 8 Voices. [1843—1846].
Op. 80 (Op. 8, Posth.). Sixth Quartett for Str. Instr., in F Min. [1847].
Op. 81 (Op. 9, Posth.). *Andante* in E; *Scherzo* in A Min.; *Capriccio* in E Min.; and Fugue in E flat; for Str. Instr.
Op. 82 (Op. 10, Posth.). Air with Variations, for P.F., in E flat [1841].
Op. 83 (Op. 11, Posth.). Air with Variations, for P.F. *à* 2 *mains*, in B flat.
Op. 83 *bis* (Op. 11 *bis*, Posth.). The same, *à* 4 *mains*.
Op. 84 (Op. 13, Posth.). Three Songs for Contralto Voice [1831, 1834, 1839].
Op. 85 (Op. 14, Posth.). *Sechs Lieder ohne Worte*, for P.F., Bk. 7 [1841—1845].
Op. 86 (Op. 15, Posth.). Six Songs [1837—1841].
Op. 87 (Op. 16, Posth.). Second Quintett for Str. Instr. (2 *Viole*), in B flat [1845].
Op. 88 (Op. 17, Posth.). Open-Air Music, six Part-Songs, for S.A.T.B. Fourth Set [1839—1844].
Op. 89 (Op. 18, Posth.). *Heimkenr aus der Fremde* (" Son and Stranger "), *Singspiel*, in one act.
Op. 90 (Op. 19, Posth.). Fourth Symphony, generally known as the " Italian Symphony," in A [1833].
Op. 91 (Op. 20, Posth.). Psalm xcviii., for Eight Voices and Orch. [1844].
Op. 92 (Op. 21, Posth.). *Allegro brillante*, for P.F., *à* 4 *mains*, in A [1841].
Op. 93 (Op. 22, Posth.). Music to the *Œdipus in Colonos* of Sophocles, for Chorus of Male Voices and Orch. [1845].
Op. 94 (Op. 23, Posth.). Scena, *Infelice*, for Sopr. Solo with Orch. [First version, 1834 ; second version, 1843].
Op. 95 (Op. 24, Posth.). Overture to Vict. Hugo's Play, *Ruy Blas* [1839.]
Op. 96 (Op. 25, Posth.). Hymn, for Alto Solo, Chorus, and Orch. [1840—1843.]
Op. 97 (Op. 26, Posth.). *Christus*,[1] Fragments of an unfinished Oratorio.
Op. 98*a* (Op. 27*a*, Posth.). *Loreley*,[2] Finale to the First Act of an unfinished Opera, Solo and Chorus.
Op. 98*b* (Op. 27*b*, Posth.). *Loreley, Ave Maria*, for Soprano Solo, and Chorus of Female Voices, from the unfinished Opera.

[1] See page 130. [2] See pages 123, 130.

Op. 98c (Op. 27c, Posth.). *Loreley*, Vintage Chorus, for Male Voices, from the unfinished Opera.
Op. 99 (Op. 28, Posth.). Six Songs [1841—1845].
Op. 100 (Op. 29, Posth.). Four Part-Songs [1839—1844].
Op. 101 (Op. 30, Posth.). The "Trumpet Overture," in C.
Op. 102 (Op. 31, Posth.). *Sechs Lieder ohne Worte*, for P.F., Bk. 8 [1845—1847].
Op. 103 (Op. 32, Posth.). *Trauer-Marsch*, in A Min., for the Funeral of Burgnüller.
Op. 104 (Op. 33, Posth.). Three Preludes, and Three Studies, for P.F.
Op. 105 (Op. 34, Posth.). Sonata, for P.F., in G min. [1821].
Op. 106 (Op. 35, Posth.). Sonata, for P.F., in B min. [1827].
Op. 107 (Op. 36, Posth.). Fifth Symphony, known as "The Reformation Symphony" in D.
Op. 108 (Op. 37, Posth.). March, for Orchestra, in D.
Op. 109 (Op. 38, Posth.). *Lied ohne Worte*, for P.F. and Cello, in D.
Op. 110 (Op. 39, Posth.). Sextett for P.F. and Str. Instr. (with 2 *Viole*), in D [1824].
Op. 111 (Op. 40, Posth.). *Tu es Petrus*, Chorus for Five Voices with Orch. [1827].
Op. 112 (Op. 41, Posth.). Two Sacred Songs.
Op. 113 (Op. 42, Posth.). Concerted Piece for Clarinet, Corno di Bassetto, and P.F. in F [1833].
Op. 114 (Op 43, Posth.). Concerted Piece for Clarinet, Corno di Bassetto, and P.F., in D Min.
Op. 115 (Op. 44, Posth.). Two Sacred Choruses for Male Voices.
Op. 116 (Op. 45, Posth.). Funeral Hymn, for Male Voices.
Op. 117 (Op. 46, Posth.). *Album-Blatt* (*Lied ohne Worte*), for P.F., in E Min.
Op. 118 (Op. 47, Posth.). *Capriccio* for P.F., in E.
Op. 119 (Op. 48, Posth.). *Perpetuum mobile*, for P.F., in C.

The following Compositions are printed without *Opus*-numbers [3]:—

Hymn, "Hear my Prayer," for Soprano Solo, and Chorus. First version with Organ Accomp.; second version with Orch. (Ded. to W. Taubert) [1844].
Hymn, *Verleih uns Frieden* ("Grant us Thy Peace"), for Chorus and Orch. (Ded. to President Verkenius).
Three Hymns, for Alto Solo, and Chorus (one taken from Op. 96).

[3] Those marked * are included in "Albums," and other similar collections.

Kyrie Eleison, for Double Chorus [1846].
*Anthem, "Lord, have Mercy," for Voices only, in A Min.
Festgesang, for Male Voices and Orch.
**Ersatz für Ueberstand*, for Four Male Voices.
Song, "The Garland" (words by T. Moore) [1829].
*Two Songs, "There be none of beauty's daughters," and "Sun of the sleepless" [1834].
Three *Volkslieder*, for Two Voices, with P.F. Accomp.
Song, *Warnung vor dem Rhein*.
Song, *Des Seemanns Scheidelied*.
Song, *Des Mädchens Klage*.
Part-Song, *Nachtgesang*, for Four Male Voices.
Part-Song, *Die Stiftungsfeier*, for Four Male Voices.
Two Songs [1835].
Two Songs [1841].
*Étude for P.F., in F Min.
*Scherzo and *Capriccio* for P.F., in F sharp Min.
Scherzo for P.F., in B Min.
**Andante Cantabile*, and *Presto agitato*, for P.F., in B. [1838].
*Prelude and Fugue for P.F., in E Min. [Prelude, 1841; Fugue, 1827].
Zwei Clavierstücke, in B flat and G Min.
Lied auf einer Gondel, for P.F., in A [1837].
Duo Concertante, Variations on the March in *Preciosa*, for P.F., à 4 *mains*, composed in conjunction with Moscheles.
Two Sketches, for P.F.
Præludium, for the Organ, in C Min. [1841]. Published at Edinburgh in facsimile, and not included in Messrs. Breitkopf and Härtel's catalogue.
Quartett for Str. Instr., in E flat. [1823]. Published in Berlin, but not included in the Thematic Catalogue. The autograph of this early work is preserved in the British Museum.

The green volumes mentioned at page 13, contain, among other works, the original autographs of 5 unpublished Operas; 3 Sacred Cantatas; 1 Sæcular Cantata; innumerable Motets, Songs, and other vocal pieces; 11 Symphonies for Str. Instr., and 1 for Full Orchestra; Concertos for P.F.; a Concerto for Two P.Fs.; Concertos for the Violin; a Trio for P.F., Violin, and Viola; 2 Sonatas for the P.F.; 2 Sonatas for P.F. and Violin; 1 Sonata for P.F. and Viola; 1 Sonata for P.F. and Clarinet; Fugues for Str. Instr.; Fugues for the Organ; Fugues for P.F.; Studies, Fantasias, and other compositions, of which it is impossible to give a detailed catalogue.

LONDON:
PRINTED BY GILBERT AND RIVINGTON, LIMITED,
ST. JOHN'S SQUARE.